MW01625486

PRAISE FROM READERS

Loss is something that happens so suddenly. Whether the loss was someone who was young or old, those who experience the loss are at a standstill on how to navigate during the initial shock and the aftermath. With tragedy comes a lot of reflecting and moving on. Within the first few chapters of "An Unwanted Journey," I was already crying, wondering how someone could follow through with the twists and turns of grief, especially with the author's experience. While the subject can be quite grim, Jennifer manages to find ways for her readers to find the strength to move on and rediscover the beauty of life, whether it's the life of the loved one you have lost or your own. I felt I was along for the ride; I was able to reflect, and I got a few laughs out of it when getting to know Jennifer's story (how twisted is that?). It was also refreshing to hear the testimonies of others within the book, making it feel like there were more perspectives on how people navigated or continue to navigate their "Unwanted Journey." Overall, anyone who has experienced a loss will be able to relate and reflect—the perfect combination of a good book.

—Jessi Samek

The story of "An Unwanted Journey" felt like the warm hug I've been missing out on for years. While there is never an "end" to mourning, having the right resources and someone there with you can make the road to recovery just a little easier, and Jennifer's book does just that. Her words are not just a reflection of her personal journey but a guide for anyone who may be at a loss for how to cope with their own grief or provide assistance to a loved one who is suffering. "An Unwanted Journey" is a beautifully written, moving, and educational book that reminds us of the resilience of the human spirit and the healing power of shared experiences.

—Aly C.

Jennifer's story is so beautifully written. It read as if I were sitting across from her, having coffee, and listening to her story. I was transported through every page, feeling, and emotion. The information and resources she offers so that others may navigate through their loss is a true testament to her own experiences and wanting to help others. It is informative, thought-provoking, and a reminder to take nothing for granted. I thank her for sharing her story with the world. It will help and comfort many. It's a beautiful way to honor her beloved husband's life, her courage, and their love.

—Joseph Bogart

An "Unwanted Journey" describes the author's journey after her late husband unexpectedly died. She paints an elaborate picture of the events leading up to and after her husband's passing and the struggles associated with his death. I particularly appreciated how the concepts in this book applied to me, even though I have not experienced the tragic and sudden death of a loved one. The author conveys her story conversationally and realistically, including tips and suggestions on tasks one could incorporate before and after losing a loved one. The author's intention for writing this book was to help others, and she accomplishes this goal by providing educational concepts useful to almost anyone and creating a heartfelt connection with those experiencing similar loss. I did have an emotional response as I imagined losing my husband, causing me to cherish what I have and focus on essential issues. Overall, I highly recommend this book since it's an excellent tool for coping with the aftermath of loss and an inspirational example of someone courageously sharing her complicated story to support others.

—Evelyn Lewis

This book is so beautifully written. Jennifer takes us with her on this heartfelt, painful, and courageous journey, feeling her emotions every step of the way. I felt as though I was sitting next to her at times, even bringing a tear to my eye more than once at the moments when she was driving to the cemetery and the song that played while toasting the anniversary of her and her late husband's engagement. This book also includes invaluable information for someone who has lost a loved one. I give it five stars!

—Robert Varley

Jennifer's story is full of heartfelt details about the process of losing the person she loved most. She offers a balance of emotional introspection and practical, helpful details for anyone going through a similar loss or for anyone supporting a loved one through it. I, too, became a widow in my mid-30s, so I understand being a part of this "club" in which you never,

ever want membership. Her story rings true for so many of the unexpected pieces of this devastating experience. She bravely gives us insight into her heart-wrenching journey while also considering the information that will most help others. You never think about the details you'll have to face, like writing an obituary, closing accounts, or picking up a box of ashes. Jennifer shares the emotional aspects of these things but also provides practical tools and solutions for these hurdles. The thoughtful questions and journaling pages also help the reader take Jennifer's experiences and apply them to the reader's own life to create reflection and action. Not only do I share the personal aspect of this experience, but as a health and wellness coach, I cannot stress enough the importance of self-care during these difficult times, which Jennifer highlights well. This book offers a helpful and hopeful roadmap to anyone going through the impossible journey of grieving someone close to you.

—Deanna Clauson

There are so many elements that I really appreciated in Jennifer's book, and her ability to share her journey is remarkable. Many poignant messages resonated with me that I am confident will also resonate with other readers of this book. It was apparent that she was so honoring to whoever reads this, and I feel that it's something that everyone should have in their home because death, tragedy, and loss are part of the human experience, and many of us don't know how to navigate it. I recommend it as a preemptive guide that everybody should read, not just those who have experienced loss but anybody who will.

—Jessica Ste. Michelle

AN UNWANTED JOURNEY

Embracing Life After Loss

JENNIFER NILSEN

An Unwanted Journey
Jennifer Nilsen

ISBN: 978-1-956193-80-0
Book Design & Publishing done by:
Global Book Publishing
www.globalbookpublishing.com

This book is dedicated to anyone who has suffered a loss. May you continue to move forward in your grief one day at a time.

TABLE OF CONTENTS

WELCOME

When I started writing this book, I just wanted to help others. One of my friends had invited me to interview on her podcast about my experience with the sudden traumatic loss of my husband, Jack. In the wake of the comments received after the podcast went live, it became clear that I had a lot of helpful information to share. I have been on quite the journey, and I felt that sharing my story and the lessons I have learned may help others who have gone or are going through similar experiences. Over time, it has evolved into much more than I had ever thought. Putting my story into words has been challenging at times, but also a cathartic experience for me, and I hope that it will help those either struggling with a sudden traumatic loss or are connected to someone who is.

I never really thought I would become an author. However, I've always been a writer in some ways. I loved to write short stories as a child and poems as a teenager. I have also written copy for blogs, newsletters, and social media as part of my career in marketing. But nothing to this extent. I was on a flight home from a vacation when I started writing this book, and without any outline or plan, I just typed whatever came to mind. I didn't put it in any particular order or focus on it too hard. I just let my thoughts flow. It didn't happen overnight. It took over six years. Occasionally, during the process, I would recall a memory or a story that I thought would be good to include, and then I would add it and move on to something else. It was like journaling, in a way. I had to give myself grace for the times when I didn't feel like writing. When you've suffered a loss like this, sometimes it isn't easy to even think about what happened, let alone tell someone else about it. Sometimes, it's too much, and that's okay. Eventually, it got easier, and the end goal became my beacon. In my heart, I knew that this would help people and that Jack would be proud of me for turning tragedy into something positive.

In the past, I have always felt some level of self-preservation that prevented me from openly sharing this. I will be the first to tell you that the first few pages of this story are not pretty, and to this day, I still get a little anxious when I share my story with someone for the first time. Honestly, I don't know that it will ever be easy, but I get more comfortable with it as time passes. I hope opening up about my experience may help lessen some heartache and pain for anyone who has lost someone suddenly and tragically and maybe even bring some peace and comfort in knowing they are not alone. I also hope it may help people who have not directly experienced something like this to better understand and empathize with those who have.

I am not an expert and don't have all the answers. I'm simply sharing what I have learned based on my own experience. I realize that anyone who has gone through tragic loss has a different story to tell, but in sharing our stories, I think we can all find something that connects us.

In this book, I will share with you:

- How I navigated through the first few hours and weeks of sudden traumatic loss
- Managing the administrative processes involved with an Estate and the importance of a Will
- How to accept and ask for help
- How to handle the discomfort when people don't know what to say or do for you
- The importance of self-care
- How to find a therapist right for you
- Lessons I learned on this journey

Thank you so much for reading this, having an open mind, and being willing to join me (and others who have shared their stories in this book) on this journey. If you are grieving after the unexpected, tragic death of a loved one, I am so sorry for your loss, your pain, and your grief. The simple fact that you picked up this book makes you so brave. While I can never put myself in your shoes or say I know how you feel, I can relate to what you are going through. I empathize with your situation; my heart and condolences go out to you. I wish you strength, courage, and bravery as you navigate life without your loved one.

A Note About the Journal Pages

Throughout this book, journal pages have been provided for you to jot down your thoughts and feelings, take note of things you find interesting, or write down something you'd like to refer back to or reflect upon later. While some prompts and questions have been provided for inspiration, these journal pages are entirely yours. You can even doodle, sketch, or write a shopping list on them. And if you don't want to use them or don't feel comfortable with them, then you don't have to use them at all. You can skip over them if it's not something you're interested in or comfortable with. It is your space to do what feels best for you, and no one can decide that for you. Remember, this is your journey, and these are your boundaries.

Wishing you much comfort and peace,
Jennifer

What do you hope to gain/learn from this book? What would help you the most?

One

OUR STORY

Before I share the story of how I lost Jack, it might be helpful for you to learn a little bit about him and our life together. He and I met on a blind date a mutual friend set us up on. At the time, he was approaching the first anniversary of starting his own business and was a one-man-show for the most part, so he was working a lot, but we still managed to spend a lot of time together. After a few short weeks, we moved in together. We were engaged after six months and married the following year. When we first got together, we lived in a little 910-square-foot rambler in the city, and after we got married, we decided to sell the house and move to the suburbs. Later that year, we found the home where we built our life together for almost ten years. We lived there until the day that he passed away.

Our daily life together was pretty typical. Jack worked very hard building his business, and I also worked full-time, so the weeknights were low-key. We would have dinner and maybe watch a movie or whatever popular reality TV show was running at the time (he LOVED reality TV). We weren't keen on large gatherings. So, on weekends, we would go out for dinner, see a movie, or take a day trip somewhere. He loved to golf and would play whenever he had the chance. He was also a huge sports fan, and catching games on TV was one of his favorite pastimes. He didn't take much vacation time from work, but we usually took a long weekend trip somewhere when he did. Our favorite travel spot was the Oregon coast. It was a place that meant a lot to him; in fact, it was where he proposed.

Jack was very giving and was always doing for others. He didn't just care for me; he was good to everyone and was the kind of person who would help anyone. He was good to our families, our friends, his employees, and, as you will read about later, even to strangers. He had a very kind heart and was loved by so many.

Then, one day, his life ended. Just like that. In an instant. Like a blackout.

In a matter of minutes, my life was changed forever. I lost my husband, home, and life as I knew it. For me, the first year and a half was undoubtedly the most challenging time of my life, not only due to the loss but all the unexpected that came in the aftermath. I think for anyone who has suffered any loss, there is no road map to tell you what to do after your loved one is gone. There is no way of knowing how you will handle it. Sometimes, very acute reminders of the loss may unexpectedly blindside you. Sometimes, it feels like a punch in the gut or a lump in the throat; other times, it can bring happiness and even laughter. These moments may reopen wounds in the healing process and bring out emotions you never knew you had. These are moments that we can't prepare for. I am about to share how I dealt with those moments, how I got through them, and how I keep moving forward and found happiness in my life again.

Two

UNEXPECTED MOMENTS

The night after Jack passed away, I experienced something that I was not expecting. I realized I had started sleeping on his side of the bed. I loosely use the term "sleeping" because I barely slept for about three weeks after he died. I spent most nights lying in my niece's bed at my sister's house, restlessly watching reruns of *Will & Grace* and waiting for the morning to arrive. Nonetheless, subconsciously, I think his side of the bed seemed more comforting than mine. I wanted to feel his presence even though I wasn't sleeping in our bed and Jack was no longer beside me. This would be the beginning of many unexpected moments.

Three

OUR LAST WORDS

Our last phone call lasted 5 minutes and 8 seconds.

I had left work and called Jack on my way home, just as I did every day. I asked him how his day had been. I told him that I had had lunch with my sister, and we had discussed having a party for all our family's March and April birthdays. I told him I was thinking about stopping by my mom's house on my way home because she had just returned from a month-long trip visiting her family in Norway the night before. It may seem inconsequential to recount what we talked about that day. But we spoke every day after work. We had thousands of conversations that I don't remember. But I remember this one vividly. I can't unhear it.

Suddenly, I heard Jack pull away from the phone to greet his uncle, Bill, which was a surprise because he hadn't been in touch for a while. Then I heard Jack exclaim, "Are you crazy?!"

He started screaming. I heard some commotion, and the phone went dead.

It was one of the most surreal moments I've ever experienced in my entire life. I remember feeling paralyzed as I tried to make sense of what was happening. I didn't know what to do except to try and call him back. I called him on his cell phone and got no answer, then on his office line, and again it went to voice mail. I anxiously waited at a stoplight for the light to turn green so I could get to a safe place to pull my car over, then pulled my car into the nearest parking lot I could get to and dialed 9-1-1. When the operator answered, I told her I had just been on the phone with my husband and thought he had been attacked. I gave her the address to his office and told her whom he had greeted while we were on the phone. I waited for a few minutes, which seemed like an eternity before I couldn't wait any longer, and I called 9-1-1 back to see if I could find out what was going on.

The operator assured me that help was on the way. I called back a couple more times because I had become extremely panicked. My heart was beating so hard and fast that I wondered if I might need medical attention. I've never had a heart attack, but I was afraid that at that moment, I might have one. I was in a strip mall parking lot and recalled having difficulty staying in one space. I drove around, moving from space to space, waiting for someone to call me back and tell me what was happening. I finally received a call from a detective who told me that my husband had been rushed to the hospital and that I needed to get there right away. I asked her what had happened, and she told me Jack had been shot.

I felt utterly paralyzed and too distraught to drive. So, I called my younger brother and asked if he could pick me up and take me to the hospital. It would take about 20 minutes for him to get to me, and while I was waiting for him, I decided that I needed to call my husband's mom. I will never be able to express how horrible it was to make that call.

I tried calling her on her cell phone, but she didn't answer. Then I called her landline, and her boyfriend answered. I asked to speak with her. When she came on the line, I was so distraught and shaky that I could hardly breathe the words out of my mouth to tell her that her son had been shot. She was in complete distress, unable to speak, and immediately returned the phone to her boyfriend. I didn't know much at that point, so I texted them the detective's number so they could contact her directly. Jack's mom and boyfriend lived about 85 miles from the hospital he had been taken to, so I can only imagine how helpless they must have felt making that long drive to get to him.

My sister-in-law called me shortly after that because she had just heard the news from her mom. I was speaking with her when another call came through from the detective. At the same time, my brother had just pulled into the parking lot to pick me up. I switched calls to speak with the detective, and she asked me if I was with my brother as I was frantically trying to grab everything I could from my car and get into my brother's truck.

When I got into the passenger seat, the detective told me my husband did not make it.

It isn't easy to put into words how to describe that moment. Hopeless, devastating, frightening. I was lost. I immediately felt as if I was having an out-of-body experience. It wasn't real. This could not be happening. It was a nightmare. What was worse was that Bill had fled the scene and was on the loose, which gave me a horrible sense of fear. I didn't feel like he would come after me, but the fear that he was out there, armed with a gun, and no one knew his whereabouts was enough. The detective asked me to turn off my phone's location status and deactivate all our social media accounts so that the local media could not try to contact me. I was numb, yet somehow, I was able to log into our accounts and deactivate them.

How to Memorialize, Deactivate, or Close a Social Media Account for a Deceased Loved One

For guidance, use the links in the footnotes for each social media platform:

Facebook

- Legacy Contacts[1]

Instagram

- Memorialize Account[2]

LinkedIn

- Memorialize or Close Account[3]

[1] https://www.facebook.com/help/991335594313139/?helpref=hc_fnav
[2] https://help.instagram.com/264154560391256
[3] https://www.linkedin.com/help/linkedin/answer/a1336663

Twitter

- Deactivate or Close Account[4]

TikTok

- Request Account Removal[5]

Google/YouTube

- Request Account Closure[6]

The detective told me we needed to meet so that she could ask me some questions. She told me to pick somewhere I felt safe and that she would meet me there. So I had my brother take me to a police station. I walked inside the station lobby and picked up a telephone on the wall to get assistance. I explained to the woman who answered the phone that I was there to meet with a detective to speak about the murder of my husband. My brother waited with me for a couple of minutes until I heard a clicking sound, and the door to a secured area was opened. I was greeted by a police officer who escorted me back into a small conference room, where I sat and waited until the detective arrived. It felt cold, sterile, and empty. I sat alone in a chair at a conference table in this monochromatic room for what seemed like an eternity.

[4] https://help.twitter.com/en/forms/account-access/deactivate-or-close-account/deactivate-account-for-deceased

[5] https://www.tiktok.com/legal/report/feedback

[6] https://support.google.com/accounts/troubleshooter/6357590?hl=en

When the detective arrived, she entered with Jack's mom and boyfriend. I don't remember what I said or did when I saw them. I remember thinking, "What do you say to a mother who has just lost her son?" They stayed briefly and then left so the detective and I could talk privately. I was interviewed for about an hour, recounting what had happened and answering questions about my late husband and anything I knew about his family, friends, employees, and Bill.

We looked at social media pages and scrolled through the entire contact list on my phone, trying to pinpoint anyone who might be a helpful source of information for the detective. The detective showed me a copy of the alert that would be distributed to all law-enforcement agencies, with Bill's driver's license photo and a picture of his vehicle. I could hardly even look at it. It felt surreal, but this wasn't a crime show or movie; it was real life.

The detective hugged me before she left. She told me that if I needed anything, even a piece of chocolate cake in the middle of the night, she would get it to me. I have not forgotten how comforted that moment made me feel. I'd never felt so helpless in my entire life. I had no idea what I was going to do. I walked out into the lobby of the police station, and it felt like a shell, much in the same way that I was feeling inside. I felt like I had a big gaping hole in the center of my chest. I felt heavy and tired, but I was not able to relax.

My younger brother had been waiting for me, and my niece's husband had also arrived. He took me to his and my niece's house for the night. The car ride home was full of devastating phone calls. I remember speaking with my mom and my sister. I called my closest girlfriends. Some of whom I was able to reach, while others I waited anxiously to receive a call back from. It was late evening, so some people had already gone to bed. Once the alert had been sent out by law enforcement, Jack's murder became a news story. So my only hope was that I would get a hold of everyone I needed to before they heard about it on the news rather than hearing it directly from me. I was on the other end of the shock, repeatedly playing in my ear. Everyone I spoke with was in complete disbelief, often pausing in silence. In that silence, I could "hear" them trying to process the tragic reality of what I was saying.

For the next few days, I avoided all news coverage. Each report flashed exterior images of the building where Jack's business was located, cordoned off by yellow crime scene tape. Images flashed across the screen of Bill's photo, the vehicle he fled in, and the license plate number. I only needed to see it once for it to be permanently burned into my mind.

The detective warned me that members of my family and I might be contacted directly by reporters. She said they can be relentless and may try to contact me via phone, social media, or even show up on my front lawn. She gave me her card and instructed me to have them contact her directly if that happened. The thought of it just made me feel sick and disgusted. How unbelievably insensitive could they possibly be? I immediately notified my entire family not to speak with anyone or mention anything about what was happening on their social media accounts. It would make it more difficult for the media to contact us and help to protect the investigation. I did not want anything to keep this horrible human being from being caught and put behind bars as quickly as possible. Thankfully, I was not contacted; however, my sister was. A representative from one of the local news stations messaged her via Facebook, and she ignored and deleted the message.

The ripple effect of this tragedy continued to grow within the first few hours as several people who knew Jack and Bill needed to be contacted and, in some cases, brought to safety as a precautionary measure. We had no idea where Bill was or where he would be headed next. There is no way to determine what someone like this is capable of or what lengths they will go to do it. He had driven several hours, committed the crime, got back in his van, and drove all those hours back to where he lived. But because we weren't sure if he had left the area at the time, the detective requested that I contact my boss and ask her to close the office the following day and ask everyone to work from home as another precaution until Bill was located and captured. I felt terrible for the hassle and inconvenience my boss and co-workers were being put through, but it made me feel a bit more relieved to ensure their safety.

Four

THE LONGEST NIGHT

Once I settled in at my niece's house, I was up most of the night handling phone calls. Feeling anxious about Bill's whereabouts, I would get up from time to time to look out the window. He did not know my niece and had no idea where she lived, so it didn't seem to make any sense as to why I was doing this. I can only blame the feelings I was experiencing on the post-traumatic stress disorder I was dealing with in the wake of this tragedy. The detective told me I should stay somewhere for the night where I felt safe and that Bill did not know about. She would have helped me find somewhere safe to stay if I had no option, but thankfully, I had a place to stay with people who made me feel comfortable.

Late into the evening, I received a call from the medical examiner's office. At first, I didn't pick up the call and let it roll to voice mail. I didn't know the number, and I typically don't answer calls from people I don't know, but in this case, I was even more hesitant due to the current circumstances. So, I called the detective and had her verify the legitimacy, and once confirmed, I called him back.

He wanted to ask me about Jack's medical and health history for organ donation. I was asked about a hundred questions that took approximately one hour to complete. For the final question, he wanted to know if there was anyone who I thought might object to Jack's remains being used for organ donation or research. While I didn't think anyone would have an issue with it, for some reason, I felt compelled to double-check with his mom to ensure she would be okay with it. This was her son, and I didn't feel it would be right to decide without asking her. I was feeling the weight of this decision, knowing that I wasn't all together emotionally, and I didn't want to be fully responsible for making such a big decision.

It was two or three o'clock in the morning, and I wasn't sure if I would get a hold of her, but I asked the medical examiner if I could call Jack's mom to confirm and then call him back. I called her, and she, like me, was not sleeping and immediately picked up the phone. I asked her, and she had no objections. I called the medical examiner to let him know so he could complete the questionnaire. I never thought in a million years that I would find myself speaking with a medical examiner in the middle of the night about my late husband's remains, but enduring that turned out to be a true miracle for someone, and I'll share that story a little later.

What Do I Need to Know About Organ Donation?

- You can become an organ donor when you get/renew a driver's license or by registering online.[7]
- There is no age limit to become an organ donor.
- Health at the time of death helps to determine which organs and tissues can be donated and transplanted.
- There is no cost for organ donation.
- If you do not register as an organ donor, your family can consent to donate your organs and tissue on your behalf.

Resources:

- Donate Life America[8]
- Health Resources & Services Administration—OrganDonor.gov[9]

My niece and her husband had a newborn baby at home, my great-niece, who was just six weeks old, almost to the day of Jack's death. The last photo I have, or anyone has, of Jack is of him holding her. He and I are her great-aunt, great-uncle, and godparents. Jack was so excited when they announced they were pregnant. He was not much of a shopper, but he was so excited that he wanted to go to the children's clothing store at the mall

[7] https://www.organdonor.gov/sign-up
[8] https://donatelife.net/
[9] https://www.organdonor.gov/

and buy an outfit for her when she was born. She was wearing that outfit in that last photo, the only photo of them together.

As early morning approached, my great-niece awoke, and my niece fed and changed her, then handed her to me. I rested her on my chest, and she fell back to sleep. It is a moment I will never forget. I felt she was an angel sent to comfort me at one of the worst times of my life. I have heard that a rebirth of life is brought into the world when one leaves this earth, and this may have been a perfect example of that. My great-niece gave me so much joy and peace, and it was a blessing that she was born when she was. She gave me a reason to keep moving forward. I knew Jack would want me to continue to be there for her on behalf of both of us. The time I spent with her over the next year, the time I have continued to spend with her, and the siblings who have since joined her have been a huge part of the healing process for me.

At about 6:00 a.m., a dear friend of both Jack and me, whom I had tried to get a hold of the night before, called me back. We typically didn't speak at this time of day, so I could immediately tell in her voice when I picked up the phone that she knew something was wrong. When I told her what had happened to Jack, as expected, she was in complete shock and disbelief. I recounted a bit more about what had happened. She immediately offered to call Jack's best friend, who was a mutual friend of ours as well, to share the news. They were with us the night that Jack and I first met and were friends long before I knew Jack, so this was extremely tough for them to take.

Later that morning, another dear friend picked me up to take me to meet with Jack's family. I was advised not to drive, at least not for the first few days, because I was struggling with so many emotions and may not be as alert, especially since I had not slept much. I could not return to our house because Bill knew where we lived, and he had yet to be located. So, our first stop was a store where I could pick up a few essential items to get me through the next few days. I only had the outfit I had worn to work the day Jack died. My niece had loaned me some pajamas, a clean pair of underwear, and a shirt to wear in the meantime because I wasn't sure how long I would be without my personal belongings.

My friend then took me to Jack's aunt and uncle's house, where a few of his family members had gathered. We were joined by Lew Cox, who was the Executive Director of an organization called Violent Crime Victim Services at the time. He had been referred to us by a neighbor who knew him through their experience with sudden traumatic loss. Sadly, Mr. Cox's work resulted from his personal experience with sudden traumatic loss when his daughter was murdered. He started the organization to help others in similar situations.

I don't remember much about our conversation that day, but I was grateful that he took the time to be there with us and share his book, *Coping with Traumatic Death: Homicide*. It is very relatable and gave me a sense of comfort in knowing that someone else had gone through something similar to what I was experiencing. Soon after he left, I called a funeral home and church to set up appointments for the next day to start preparations for the memorial service.

Funeral Planning Resources

How to Find a Funeral Home Near Me

- Legacy.com—Funeral Homes[10]

How to Write an Obituary

- Legacy.com—How to Write an Obituary[11]
- Legacy.com—Free Obituary Writing Tool[12]

---

[10] https://www.legacy.com/funeral-homes/
[11] https://www.legacy.com/advice/how-to-write-an-obituary/
[12] https://obituary.legacy.com/obitwriter-free-ai-tool/?gad=1&gclid=Cj0KC-QjwwvilBhCFARIsADvYi7K2UBfR8Qm88xUNaAP-_O_NFsBwZ3ps-Jm-Vpymei3NVR3QOZ7NQlOMaAp-vEALw_wcB

Five

THE FIRST FORTY-EIGHT

The first forty-eight hours were the longest hours of my life. I could not sleep, and everything made me nervous. Every sound made me jump. Every phone call gave me anxiety. Jack's uncle had been driving a white van, so every white van I passed on the road or saw in a parking lot gave me the chills.

After meeting with the family, my friend took me to a Mexican restaurant for a late lunch. I didn't feel like eating, but I had to try. Shortly after we sat down, a man who looked exactly like Bill walked into the restaurant with a boy who looked to be about twelve years old. I couldn't think of anyone in Jack's family who fit the young boy's description, but the man with him, to me, looked exactly like his uncle. I quickly excused myself to the restroom, texted my friend, and told her we had to leave the restaurant immediately. I was frantic, and my heart was racing. I got in the car and tried to call the detective first, but she didn't answer, so I called 9-1-1.

I told the operator that my husband had been murdered the day before and I thought I had just seen the man who did it. She immediately connected me with a police officer. I remember telling him I thought it was odd that he would be at a restaurant the day after committing a crime like that. Still, the detective had told me to contact her or the police if I saw or remembered *anything*, and the officer assured me that strange things had happened.

Two officers were dispatched to the restaurant, and I was told I would receive a call back once they confronted the man I had described. I waited with bated breath for the phone to ring, and several minutes later, the call came. The officer told me that the man was, in fact, not Bill. They reassured me that I was not crazy for thinking it could have been him because when the officers walked into the restaurant with a picture of Bill in hand, they immediately identified the man I had mistaken him for. They agreed that he looked very much like him.

Thankfully, the man was very accommodating. When they apologized for disrupting his meal, he joked that he would have an interesting story to tell when he got home. Bless that man for not being upset about this case of mistaken identity. It was more evidence of post-traumatic stress disorder (PTSD) that, unfortunately, was becoming more common for me. I was a lot more cautious than usual. I did not like being alone, and I lived in fear. It is something that I don't think I will ever completely overcome. However, I can say that the symptoms are far less severe now than they were initially.

The following day, my friend drove me to meet with the pastor at the church. Jack's sister, mom, and her boyfriend met us there. The church was just minutes from the house where Bill used to live. I knew that he knew the area well. Since he had not yet been located, I experienced what I could only guess was a panic attack at the thought that maybe he was hiding somewhere nearby. It was an intensely emotional experience for me. I started crying and didn't make it more than a few minutes into our meeting before I had to leave and reschedule to meet with the pastor a couple of days later. PTSD had reared its ugly head yet again.

In a way, I think it worked out that I had an opportunity to meet with the pastor on my own. It felt like a much-needed therapy session. We spoke at length about Jack. Many people who attended the memorial service asked me if we were members of that church because the pastor captured who Jack was so well that it was like he knew him. He also helped prepare me for the memorial service so I would know what to expect, and he shared some helpful tips and advice.

One piece of advice he gave me that I will never forget was not to be upset or take it personally if anyone says anything that might seem inappropriate or stupid. It's not that they mean to hurt your feelings. It's just that it's difficult for people to know what to say in those moments, but they feel the need to say something, so what comes out may not always be appropriate.

I heeded his advice, but don't remember much of what anyone said at the memorial service. I only recall seeing what seemed like an endless sea of people. Besides, I would never discount anyone for what they say in these situations because it is unfathomable to process tragic events like this. It can be difficult for anyone to know what to say.

The next stop was the funeral home. I had called the day before to make the appointment, and when I walked into the reception area and told the woman at the desk who I was, she turned out to be the person I had spoken with over the phone the day before. The very first words out of her mouth after I introduced myself were, "I thought you sounded young on the phone, but I didn't realize that you were quite this young." It hit me like a rock, yet I was so numb that it didn't provoke me to respond. It was shocking for her to see a thirty-seven-year-old widow walk through the door. Remember what the pastor said about reacting to what people might say? That was well-timed advice.

The funeral director greeted us, and we walked back to his office to discuss the arrangements. I remember feeling like I was merely existing. My eyes glazed over the paperwork before me as he explained the options. He led me into a room with shelves full of various cremation urns and boxes, some bare and plain while others were more ornate and elaborate. I selected a mahogany wood box with a glossy piano finish I thought was perfect. It's difficult to explain how I can say that. I was picking out a wooden box to hold the ashes of my cremated husband.

How is that perfect? It's not. But maybe, in some strange way, I was making the best of the situation. I was trying to make myself feel less uncomfortable about the task at hand.

We returned to the funeral director's office, and I went through the motions, signing paperwork for Jack's cremation. The funeral director warned me there was a paragraph detailing the cremation process, which I signed off on but declined to read. I appreciated his efforts to protect me against something that may have triggered me and caused additional grief. I sat there watching as the costs continued to add up. The funeral director gave me pamphlets about obtaining mental health and financial assistance. It seemed so insensitive at that moment to even think about it. Who can think about money at a time like this? The loss is so significant. And yet, it's just another thing you have to deal with that you wish you didn't have to.

In those moments, I would wonder, how could this be happening? How is it possible that I could be sitting in a funeral home right now, making arrangements for my late young husband's memorial service? He was just forty-two years old at the time of his passing. The funeral director mentioned an assistance program through the state that I could apply for to pay for a portion of the funeral since another person caused my late husband's death. After filling out and sending in the paperwork and the proper documentation, I found out that I made too much money at my job (which was not a lot by any means) to qualify.

The funeral director had also informed me of a widow's benefit[13] offered through the Social Security Administration for which I applied. I filled out the paperwork and decided to take it to the office the following week. I walked in, pulled a number from the red ticket dispenser, and waited. Eventually, my number was called, and I was escorted back to a tiny cubicle at the back of the building.

The clerk collected information from me, and then I waited as she filled out and printed a document that I was to sign to receive the benefit. The clerk asked me to read over the document and sign the last page. As I skimmed through it, I was stopped in my tracks when I came to a portion of a sentence that read, "…their marriage was ended by death…"

Talk about a punch in the gut.

When your vows say, "Til death do us part," they mean it. I was a widow. I was no longer married, even though I felt just as married as I had been for almost ten years. I packed up my things, and as I left, I was told I would receive my widow's benefit for $252 deposited directly into my checking account. Honestly, I didn't feel like the amount was worth the time, effort, or pain I had felt to obtain it. It wasn't even enough to cover half the cost of one of the obituaries in the newspaper (I placed one obituary in the major city newspaper and one in the local paper in the town where Jack grew up).

[13] https://www.ssa.gov/benefits/survivors/ifyou.html

I felt so badly about how the loss of my late husband and the tragic events behind it might affect our young family members. I remember sitting on the couch with my sister and asking her if she had spoken about it with her kids and how they felt about it. She said that she and their dad had discussed it with them, and they knew they had a safe space to talk about it whenever needed. But I also wanted to speak with them. So I asked my sister if it would be okay for me to talk to them, and she agreed. I just wanted to explain to them that their uncle loved them and would not want this situation to affect them negatively. I assured them that he would like them to continue to do well in school and be successful, independent, happy adults. All of these things would honor their uncle in the best way possible.

Almost 48 hours had passed, and I was in the living room at my sister's house, where my family had gathered for dinner. My cell phone rang, I looked at the caller ID, and it was the detective. She called to inform me that Bill had been located and taken into custody.

I didn't know what to think at that moment. I was relieved but still wound up from everything that had happened over the last two days. I asked the detective if I could let my family know, and she said I could. I took the phone away from my ear and yelled to my family, "They caught him!" I knew this was far from over, but I could breathe a little easier knowing he was no longer on the run.

Six

LEGAL MATTERS

Just four days after Jack passed away, I found myself sitting in a conference room at my attorney's office. Since we did not have a Will, I had to work with an attorney immediately to obtain a Letter of Administration to have authorization to handle all matters dealing with the estate. Unfortunately, I ran into many stressful and heartbreaking situations due to the absence of a Will. I frequently had to jump through many very frustrating hurdles through the administrative process of managing Jack's Estate because not only did we not have a Will, but we did not have both of our names on everything we owned. It ultimately caused me to suffer some painful losses that could have been avoided if we had been better prepared. Of course, my situation's laws, regulations, and requirements may not apply to yours as they may differ according to various factors, including what you share with your spouse or partner and the laws where you live. However, my tale is a precautionary one for you to learn from.

I urge you to ask questions and educate yourself so you don't suffer the same trials and tribulations I did. Believe me, you'll thank me for it later.

Sadly, you can't trust anyone in these situations. People you think would never do anything to hurt you are not always who they appear to be. Not even those closest to you. I learned this the hard way. Death can bring out the absolute worst in people. They will make decisions without considering how they will make others feel or affect their relationship. Due to my situation's legal and confidential nature, I cannot disclose exact details. However, I will share a high-level version of what happened so that you get the gist of it.

Jack and I acquired some "property" during our marriage; however, we did not have both names on them. They were in his name only, and I did not know this until it was too late. Any property with both our names on it was considered community property, and those that did not were considered separate property. I chose to sell some items that were regarded as separate property. I spent a lot of my time researching their value and finding the right professionals to help me transact the sales, which meant I would be paying a fee for those sales. But I wanted to ensure I was selling them for a fair price. I had someone make me an offer on one of the items before I had done my research, and I found out that I would have sold it for half of what it was worth if I had agreed to that offer, which would have been an expensive mistake.

Immediately after Jack died, a "Notice to Creditors" was placed in the newspaper, a public notice filed by the estate executor to alert creditors and debtors of the death of someone. In my case, a three-month timeline was given to anyone who saw this notice and had outstanding balances to collect from the estate. It was a day or two before the deadline, and my attorney called me. I was at work and wasn't expecting a call from him. I answered the phone, and he sighed and said, "I am sick to my stomach with what I am about to tell you."

My heart dropped, and my stomach began to ache.

He told me he had received a call from another attorney representing someone who would receive half of the proceeds from the separate property items I was selling. I could not believe it. I struggled to contain myself as my eyes welled up with tears, and I asked my attorney if I could call him back. I ran out to my car and proceeded to cry harder than I'd ever cried in a very long time. I had to wait until I could regain composure and called my attorney back to confirm what he had told me. It was all legal and true. The thing is, this person didn't have to do what they did. They were not forced to do what they did. It was not required. They chose to do what they did. What's worse is they didn't think I would find out. I was the freaking executor and administrator of the estate! How would I not find out?!

I felt like I was being violently kicked while I was already down. It was one of the worst moments in my life. And what made it even more difficult was that I decided to keep quiet until all estate matters were complete and the probate was closed. I didn't want to suffer any more loss. I didn't want to endure any more heartache. I questioned how much more I could take. So, the less anyone knew, the better.

I was managing all of the payments requested from the estate. I remember the day I received the paperwork stating the amounts for each check that needed to be written to the individual for the separate property transactions. They were rather large checks, so I went to the bank to have cashier's checks made out to them. I approached a young woman who asked how she could help. I placed the paperwork on the desk and told her I needed checks in the indicated amounts. Upon review, she said, "Wow! Someone is making out like a bandit!" No kidding. It was pretty insensitive of her to say that, but I could do nothing about this awful situation unless I wanted to try and fight it in court, but that would have only ended in more loss. I just wanted to get the checks, send them, and be done with it, and hoped there would not be further monetary bleeding in the process.

I waited almost five years before I confronted this individual about their actions. I didn't discuss it with them in person or over the phone. I wrote a very emotional letter explaining how what they did hurt me. I'd kept it to myself all this time, but I could no longer pretend to have a relationship with them. It was all a lie. Everything that Jack and I had ever done for this person had been a complete waste of our time. Some may think that it was a copout that I didn't speak with them about it directly, but every time I thought I could try, I would get too emotional, and I wanted to be able to get all of my thoughts out clearly and not forget anything that I wanted to say in the process. I have not heard from this individual since I sent the letter, which to me, speaks volumes. Sadly, it took something like this to learn what kind of a person they really are.

So now you can see why my advice is to make sure that you do whatever you can to protect yourself and your loved ones so that they don't suffer more heartache beyond grieving your loss. I get that it's not fun, and I know how easy it can be to make excuses for not taking care of it right now. But trust me, getting your affairs in order now is far less painful and stressful than what your loved ones will have to deal with if you don't.

I will be the first to admit that it took me some time to prepare my own Will after Jack passed away. However, surprisingly, I discovered once I got it done that I had been making it out to be a much more complicated process in my head than it was. It wasn't nearly as arduous of a task as I thought. My attorney provided me with a questionnaire, I sent him the answers, and he added the required legalese. Then, I just had to go to his office to sign it and have it notarized. It was relatively quick and painless and gave me incredible relief when it was complete.

Like Jack and I, if you are married or living with a domestic partner, you probably have at least one account that doesn't list both of your names. For example, I had my name on the cable service because I had set that up, and Jack's name was on the lawn service because he had set that up. We had separate bank accounts when we got together, and we never bothered to get a joint account simply because it seemed easier to keep it that way. But we never thought about the ramifications of what would happen if we didn't at least give each other authorization to access our accounts if one of us were to pass away.

While it may seem like it doesn't matter, it does. When you don't have both of your names on accounts, you have to prove that the account also belongs to you and that you have the authority to make changes. Sometimes, I felt like I was being treated like a criminal. As a grieving widow, it just added more salt to the wound. I can't tell you how many copies of our Marriage Certificate, Jack's Death Certificate, and the Letter of Administration for the Estate I had to provide, even for something as simple as canceling cable service.

Important Documents

- Pull together copies of your essential documents (originals, notarized copies, photocopies, digital scans) and keep them in a secure place, such as a safe, that is easily accessible to you.
- These could be Birth Certificates, Marriage certificates, mortgage documents, bank statements, etc.
- This is a good practice for any time you need to access them.

I purchased a portable file box right after Jack passed away, which I used to keep and organize important documents. I used it daily for more than a year. It contained copies of anything I thought I would need while processing the Estate and all the transactions. I also carried a notebook and pen, which I used to take notes during phone calls and meetings, and kept a running list of tasks that needed to be completed. I am a visual person, and writing things down proved very helpful as it is nearly impossible to remember everything, especially when you're grieving and have so much going on.

Everything can seem so overwhelming after the loss of a loved one. Even what may have been the simplest of tasks can feel so daunting. So be sure to write things down; that way, you won't be forced to try and remember something you need to do. Handle one task at a time. Take notes in a notebook, create a voice recording, or have a friend help you write down what you need. If you don't feel you can manage a task, ask for help. I think you'll find there are always helpers out there.

Unfortunately, I'm in a club that I never wanted to be in—"The Widow's Club"—but if there is a "silver lining" in all of this, it's that I have an opportunity to share my experiences in the hope that it may help others. I don't claim to be an expert, nor would I ever tell anyone what they should or shouldn't do or what would or wouldn't work for them. I will insert a disclaimer right now that I am not an attorney. Therefore, for anyone seeking legal advice, I would advise that you obtain the help of a legal professional. I am only sharing my thoughts and suggestions based on my experience. However, I feel I must share the knowledge that I have gained because if I can help just one person avoid the additional stress and pain that I endured or help someone feel like they are not alone in their journey, that would be the greatest gift that could come from this. Those who know me know I am a walking public service announcement for getting a Will. I don't care if you're eighteen or eighty, single or married, *please, please, please* get a Will. Get one as soon as possible. Don't put it off. I absolutely cannot stress this enough. Again, I can only speak for myself, but at the risk of sounding like a broken record, get a Will—end of PSA.

Resources to Create a Will Online

Here are a couple of resources that can be used to create a will online. I am not being paid to list or endorse these resources, nor have I used them personally. Please conduct your own research and select the service that fits your needs.

- Legal Zoom[14]
- Trust & Will[15]

[14] https://www.legalzoom.com/personal/estate-planning
[15] https://trustandwill.com/

What is one thing you can do today to start the process of getting a Will?

Seven

ANGELS AMONG US

One day shy of a week after Jack passed, I went to the mall to pick out a guest book. I also needed to find something to wear for the funeral. I walked into one of my favorite clothing stores, and within seconds, a sales associate approached me, welcomed me to the store, and asked, "Are you looking for anything particular today?" Usually, I would reply with something like, "No, I'm just looking around," or something like that, but at that moment, my eyes instantly welled with tears. I replied, "I'm looking for something to wear to my husband's funeral." It just came out like that, without a thought in my head, and I could tell the poor woman felt horrible about it. She expressed how sorry she was and got me a tissue. I remember telling her not to feel bad and that it wasn't her fault. She helped me shop for a couple of dresses, but I quickly realized that this wasn't the sort of shopping trip that I should be doing alone. So, I called a friend who dropped everything to come and help me.

I had time to spare until my friend arrived, so I headed to a stationery store to find a guest book. The store did not have the particular one I wanted in stock, but the associate told me it was available at another location downtown. I had not mentioned what I was purchasing the book for, nor did I make any comment or complain about having to go to another location to get it. Without knowing anything about what was happening in my life, the associate offered to pick it up for me that evening on his way home from work and bring it in the next day so I could pick it up there instead of driving downtown to get it. Some might call this excellent customer service, but I call him an angel. When I felt like I had no energy to do the things I had to do, he was there to help me keep moving forward.

I returned to the clothing store with my friend, who helped me pick a dress. After I completed the purchase, the associate asked if I could leave and return in a bit so she could have the dress steamed and pressed for me. Again, another angel. And these were not the only ones. I had several angels come to my rescue throughout this process, like the wonderful friends who printed the programs for the memorial service and the kind and caring woman who provided the poster-sized photo of Jack to display at the church, all the friends and family who stepped up to assist with funeral arrangements, my sister who put together a photo slide show and Jack's aunt who assembled two large boards full of photos to display at the reception after the service. Not to mention all the people who accepted my many phone calls and text messages, who let me cry and be angry, drove me around and assisted me with countless things that I couldn't do on my own. I realize I was fortunate to have so many wonderful people around me. I will never forget all the angels who helped me because I could not have gotten through so much of it without them.

I think many times in our lives, we find ourselves in situations where people offer to help, and we don't always accept it. We may be too prideful or think we can handle things ourselves. But I will tell you that this was a time when I truly needed the help, and so when people offered, I welcomed it and was ultimately grateful for it. If I can share any advice, if you are ever in a situation like this, and I do hope you never are, it would be to accept help.

As one of my dear friends said, "Just be and let others do." Have grace for those who offer help. Tasks may get done differently than you would have liked, but remember that the helpers are doing things from the heart and in the best way they know how.

Look to your friends and colleagues and consider who can help you with specific tasks.

- Know a good writer? Ask them if they would help you write an obituary or eulogy.
- Got a creative friend? Ask them if they could help create a program for the memorial service.
- Has someone offered to run errands? Have them pick up the needed items for you.

Conversely, if you want to help someone who has just lost a loved one, consider what you are particularly good at. What is your expertise? Rather than asking if or how you can help, providing some specific offers will be easier for the recipient to accept as they won't have to think of something for you to help with.

- Do you love to cook? Make some homemade meals that are easy to freeze and heat up.
- Are you a green thumb? Offer to mow the lawn or pull weeds.
- Do they have kids? Offer to take them to the park or out for ice cream.

As many people around you may not know what to say, they may not know what to do either. Giving them a task will help them feel better and take some weight and worry off your shoulders. The bottom line is don't hesitate to ask for help when needed. It will be beneficial to both you and those around you.

What do you need help with?
Who can you ask for help?

Eight

SEEKING PROFESSIONAL HELP

If it is necessary and within your means, don't be afraid to seek the assistance of professionals before making any major decisions. I enlisted the help of professionals to ensure that I had all of the details and information I needed to make intelligent and thoughtful decisions. Many times, there were things that I didn't understand or even think about until I spoke with an expert. While there may be a fee involved, it is far less costly than the mistake you make by trying to manage it on your own. In the case of Jack and I, we were lucky that we had life insurance, so in many cases, I could hire a professional as needed. My situation would have been very different if we had not had life insurance. Just the funeral costs alone would have been difficult to cover. I recommend purchasing life insurance[16]

[16] https://www.policygenius.com/

if you don't have it already. Even if you are single, even a small policy will help those needing to take care of your affairs after you are gone.

There were many things I didn't know how to do or take care of simply because I had not been in a situation like this before. I had to make several decisions I wished I could have made with Jack. For example, I sold our home, which was the first home I've ever owned, and I found selling our house difficult because he and I had bought our home together. I was lucky enough to have a fabulous real estate agent who went above and beyond to help me through it, and I am eternally grateful that I had her in my life.

I can't say I made the right decisions every time, but I certainly put forth my best effort. Based on what I went through, all I can suggest is to stop and take the time to think things through entirely before you proceed. Look at multiple options and get more than one opinion. There are people who can and will help you. If you're like me, accepting help from others can be difficult. But in my case, I am glad I did. I have heard that people who get into these situations tend to make decisions they regret later. I wanted to try and prevent that and certainly would not want it to happen to anyone else.

Thankfully, in this day and age, we have a lot of resources available to us, and a lot of them at no cost. I did a lot of my research online, and I wasn't afraid to ask questions of people I trusted and knew might have information or further insight on the things that I needed help with. Through that process, I learned a lot, was able to take control of how things were handled, and gained strength with each accomplishment, no matter how big or small. I knew in those moments that Jack would have been so proud of me for working through so many complex tasks. It was critical in many ways as it gave me the motivation I needed to continue to move in a forward motion.

Nine

MOVING FORWARD, NOT MOVING ON

I emphasize the phrase "move forward" as it is different from the words "move on." I did not feel like moving on from Jack during this process. I felt very much like I was still connected to him. In my mind, I had no other choice but to keep moving forward every single day. Jack would never have wanted me to crawl into a hole and stop living my life. He asked me to promise him that if he passed away, I would try to find someone else and not be alone. During our marriage, we talked about what would happen or what we would do if, heaven forbid, one of us were to pass away. We always told each other we would not want the other to give up. I can hear Jack saying, "You're not going down!" I've carried that with me every day since he died.

I admit some days were more difficult than others, but I honored those days and allowed them to happen. I accepted them and realized it's all part of the grieving and healing process. But I refused to let those days or anything that had happened take me down. I was unwilling to let it happen. To keep moving forward and being strong was my way of honoring my late husband in the most meaningful way possible.

Ten

GOING BACK "HOME"

One of the most difficult moments during the first week after Jack died was when I returned to our home for the first time. I don't know that I would have returned there as soon as I did. However, during my meeting with the pastor, he asked if there was anything that I would like to have at the service that belonged to Jack. There was no question that I wanted to have his favorite football jersey there. Not to mention, I was running out of clothes and wanted to get some of my toiletries and things so I didn't have to keep buying them.

The day before the service, my friend drove me to the house. The closer we got, the more I felt overcome with dread. We parked in the driveway, and it took me several minutes to get out of the car. I walked up to the door, inserted the key into the lock, and again, it took a few moments before I could open it. I slowly pressed on the door, and as I walked in, I saw Jack's shoes lined up next to the stairs. I broke down in uncontrollable tears. It was the first time I had cried hard since he died. Seeing his shoes made it all very real that he was gone.

As I scanned the house, I saw the plate and milk glass from his dinner the night before he died sitting on the kitchen counter. I immediately walked over and put them in the dishwasher. I'm unsure what made me do that, but I didn't want to look at them anymore.

The feeling I had in the house was so intense that I just wanted to get what I needed and get out of there as quickly as possible. I walked up the stairs to our bedroom. Again, the tears began to roll down my face as I pulled the jersey off the hanger, loosely folded it up, and put it in my suitcase. Then, I opened the doors to my closet. My friend helped shove as much clothing as possible into one large suitcase while I grabbed my toiletries, and we were out the door within minutes. I didn't return to our home for about a month after that.

Eleven

IN MEMORIAM

On the morning of the memorial service, I received a call from the pastor who had called to check on me to see how I was doing. I told him I was about to go up the street to the drug store to buy some pantyhose and travel-sized tissue packages to be placed in baskets next to the guest book. He advised that I should have someone else do this, but I needed the distraction. It was something to do. Sitting around and doing nothing until it was time to leave for the service was doing me no good. A few hours later, one of my dear friends picked me up, and when we arrived at the church, we, along with Jack's sister, mom, and her boyfriend, headed straight to the pastor's office in the basement, where we stayed until the service began. I remember hearing footsteps above my head as people arrived at the church—the volume of the footsteps continued to grow louder as the time of the service approached.

The pastor then gathered us in prayer before we followed him up the stairs to the front of the sanctuary to a row of seats next to the podium. I looked out at the large crowd, waiting for the service to start. I couldn't focus on anyone until I saw someone I had not seen in many years. I lunged up from my seat and walked straight to her to give her a long hug. The church was so full of people that, at this point, there was only standing room available at the back. Over three hundred people had shown up to pay their respects. I was overwhelmed. The loss we felt when Jack was taken from us extended far beyond our family and immediate circle of friends.

When the service ended, Jack's sister and I raced through the crowd to the bathroom to freshen up. We needed just a moment before we faced the crowd. When we came out of the bathroom, we were like fish trying to swim upstream, being held up by this large flow of people all making their way into the gymnasium next to the church for the reception. I noticed a basketball hoop in the gym, which Jack's sister and I agreed was fitting since Jack had grown up in the area playing basketball at the YMCA as a kid.

When we finally reached the entrance, I only made it about 10 feet into the building before I was met by a crowd of people wanting to give their condolences, share stories, give hugs, and share tears. I met so many people whom I had heard Jack speak about but had never met—strangers to me who offered to help with anything I needed. I stayed in that same spot until the last person left. I never saw the photo boards that Jack's aunt made or the slide show that my sister put together. I don't even know what kind of food was provided. The church was filled with so many bouquets that some were taken down the street to a local senior care facility and hospital for the patients to enjoy. Someone had told us this is very common when an abundance of flowers has been gifted at a funeral.

If there was one thing I came away from that day with, it was that Jack was so loved, and people who loved him were there for me like he had been there for all of them. I knew that no matter what, I would not be alone. If there was ever a time that I felt the most relief, it was immediately after the memorial service was over. In just the past ten days, I had lost my husband, feared for my life, faced the initial stages of grief and loss, planned the first funeral I'd ever planned, and started a lengthy process of dealing with the criminal justice system. I had barely slept or eaten, and even after all that, having the memorial service behind me gave me this tremendous release that I hadn't felt in days. I had laughed, cried, and connected with so many people that day, and I felt like I had taken the first steps my heart needed to begin the process of healing.

After the funeral, I met with some of my friends for coffee, who had traveled several hours from Canada to be there. I was so grateful to have them there and thoroughly enjoyed our time together. When I returned to my sister's house, a few members of my family and some friends had gathered there. As much as I appreciated them being there, I only wanted to get out of my funeral clothes into my pajamas and not be around people anymore. So, I excused myself from the gathering and went up to bed. As an empath, it was a big step for me to have been able to set that boundary and not allow myself to feel obligated to join in out of guilt. Instead, I opted to take care of myself; believe me, it was necessary.

Twelve

THIRTY-EIGHT

My 38th birthday was the day after the funeral. One of my cousins had flown in from Norway to attend and would only be in town for a couple of days. So, I decided to take him sightseeing around town that day and try to enjoy spending some time with him while he was here. While the funeral had provided me with some release, there was still a lot to get through, but I wanted to do something that gave my body and mind a short break from it all. It was a comfort to me to try and do something that made me feel "normal" again, even if it was just for one day.

You may ask yourself how I could spend a day trying to have fun a little over a week after Jack passed away. I get that. I felt guilty about it too, and imagine that it is entirely normal and probably something that others in this situation feel. But I also knew if there was any hope in my getting through the coming days, weeks, and months, I would have to allow myself time to breathe between the chaos. In this case, it involved showing my cousin around town, having lunch at a restaurant by the waterfront, and later, having Easter dinner with my family. I wasn't about to beat myself up about doing something that made me feel good. With every decision I made and every activity I engaged in, I thought about Jack and asked myself what he would do in this situation. I knew he would have wanted me to do exactly what I was doing. In so many moments of uncertainty, this was something that I was sure of. There would be plenty of time for sadness, but this day was not about that.

Three days before my late husband died, he gave me my first semi-professional camera as an early birthday gift. It took about three months to take the camera out of the box and use it. At first, it was too emotional to think about using the camera. Then I realized that if he were here, he would want me to use it. He would be hurt and disappointed that I wasn't. One of my friends mentioned that she was preparing to host a high school graduation party for her son, and many family members would be flying in from out of state. It would be the first time in several years that her family would be together again, so I offered to be the official party photographer. I arrived at her house early, took some family photos, and then stayed for the afternoon to take candid shots. I was having so much fun, and my friend was so thankful that someone was there to capture these memories since she was so busy hosting and enjoying time with her family. Since then, I have used it several times to take pictures at special events for family and friends. I know that it would mean the world to my husband that I was putting it to good use, and having that gift means the world to me.

What will you do for yourself on your birthday?

Thirteen

SELF-CARE

The week following the memorial service, I came down with a nasty cold, which didn't surprise me. I had been through the wringer, and my body had enough. I contacted my primary care provider to let her know what had happened, and she suggested I set up an appointment to come in and see her for a checkup. Sadly, after having what my doctor used to call "A+ checkups" all my life, I had been faced with my first medical condition ever, high blood pressure, which, no surprise, had most likely been brought on by the tremendous stress and anxiety that I had been struggling with. Thankfully, I found out early on, and I was able to combat it and start doing things to help keep it under control. I am thankful that I took the time for self-care and made myself aware of my current health condition so that I could do things to ensure that it did not get worse. Even if you don't think something is physically wrong with you, I highly recommend you schedule a checkup with a medical professional if you are ever in a high-stress situation like this, even if only for peace of mind. That way, if there is an issue, you can take care of it early before it has the potential to get out of hand.

After the visit with my PCP, I decided to start seeing a massage therapist regularly because, as someone prone to lower back issues that worsen during stressful situations, I needed to address it from a preventative standpoint as soon as possible. I believe it is essential, especially in times of distress, to do whatever you can to care for yourself and keep yourself healthy. My experience has been that if you don't, your body will tell you when you need to take care of yourself, hence why I got sick.

I recall one time, before the loss of Jack, when I was going through a particularly stressful time, and my back went out so severely that I could not walk for a week, crawling on all fours to go to the bathroom. I had been ignoring it and letting it get past the point of being able to remedy it before it got worse. I had to get a cortisone shot in my back and acupuncture in my hip just to get up and move again. Since then, I do not mess with caring for my back if I feel any tightness or pain. It was a harsh lesson for me to listen to my body's cues and that mental stress can affect your physical health.

Self-care comes in many forms; what works for me may not work for others. Do whatever makes you feel comfortable. Some of the other methods of self-care that I enjoyed were taking walks, watching my favorite movie with pizza delivery, having a coffee with a friend, taking weekend road trips, or dining out for a nice meal. If doing nothing is what you want to do, that's okay too. No one can decide what will work best for you but you.

I started seeing a therapist three weeks after Jack passed away. I had not been to one since my dad passed away when I was nineteen, but I know it helped, and I felt that it was something I should try again, and I wanted to start as soon as possible. I was dealing with many tough emotions, and it wasn't always easy to talk to anyone about it.

Not to mention that several people around me were also dealing with this loss, and not everyone deals with loss in the same way. Some people have no trouble discussing it, but it's difficult for others. It has been my experience that you can speak freely with a therapist, and they won't judge or get angry with you. You can't hurt their feelings or say the wrong thing. You can react however you want and say whatever you want, and they will listen and provide you with the support, insight, and tools you need to get through whatever it is that you are working on getting through. Not knowing how to find a therapist, I sought the help of the Psychology Today website, where you can search by location, insurance acceptance, etc., to find a therapist to fit your needs.

How to Find a Therapist

- Visit the Psychology Today[17] website
- Click on Find a Therapist
- Enter your City or Zip Code
- Filter the search by Issues, Insurance, Gender, Types of Therapy, Age, Price, and More

Once I narrowed it down, I set up complimentary consultations with three therapists before selecting the one I worked with, which I highly recommend. I needed to be completely comfortable with my chosen therapist, just as they would want me to be comfortable with them. Once I decided on the one I felt was the right fit, I met with her weekly for several months. I remember feeling extremely nervous and anxious as I walked into my therapist's office for our first session. But after it was over, I knew immediately that I had done the right thing for myself and everyone else around me. It was so comforting to get stuff off my chest to a neutral party in a place where I knew what I said would stay there. I remember wishing I had taken the rest of the day off after my first session because it was one of the most mentally exhausting experiences I'd had in a very long time, which made it clear to me that it was working precisely how I needed it to.

[17] https://www.psychologytoday.com/us

There were so many things that I was working through that felt so foreign, crazy, and abnormal. But my therapist was able to help me compartmentalize things when I was feeling so discombobulated. It provided me with the opportunity to say something that I usually wouldn't be comfortable speaking about with people that I knew. No one can put themselves in the shoes of others, especially in a situation like this. No matter how much you think you understand what someone is feeling, you can't. You can't feel the same, you won't grieve the same, and there is no way to process it in the same way. How you choose to grieve and heal is yours. We are all individuals; no one can tell you how to get through these things. No one.

List three things you can do to provide yourself with self-care.

Fourteen

LIVING "ALONE"

I lived with my sister for about a month after Jack passed, which I truly appreciated. After that, I was asked by a dear friend of mine if I would consider moving in with her and her boyfriend. They lived in the same neighborhood where Jack and I had our house, and it made more sense to live there because I would be in an environment that was familiar to me, near people and places I knew. It allowed me to revert to as much of my daily routine as possible.

I couldn't imagine living in our house again. That was just too emotionally difficult for me. But being back in our neighborhood felt comforting and gave me the sense of normalcy I needed. It was also convenient for me to stay near our home to check on it regularly and eventually begin the selling process.

When you find yourself in a situation where, in mere seconds, your entire life is completely changed, you search for those things that are familiar, that will provide comfort, and that will make you feel like you have some level of control.

My friend and I didn't know each other well before then, and I had never met her boyfriend. We had met in the neighborhood a few years prior and had only gotten together a few times. It wasn't until I moved in with her that our friendship developed. Knowing that we weren't that close then, I asked her later what compelled her to ask me to move in with them. She told me that she just felt like it was the right thing to do. At a time when my life was in limbo, I am grateful that she accepted me into her home and took me in as a part of her family.

They included me in everything from family dinners and birthdays to holidays and weddings. We took road trips, went to concerts, cooked meals together, and even went on a vacation to see my family in Norway. At a time when many people might have felt like they were walking on eggshells around me, my friend, her boyfriend, and their family conducted their lives as usual, and I became a welcome extension of that. They were always happy to have me there but never made me feel bad if I didn't want to participate in something. They understood that this was all a part of my grief and healing process and that sometimes, I just needed to be alone.

They celebrated with me through every mountain I overcame and consoled me when the road got bumpy, and believe me, and it got bumpy. Having that level of openness and acute sensitivity made me feel less alone. I had people who walked beside me and supported me through the loss. While my living situation may not have been considered "normal" or conventional, it worked for me and made me feel comfortable, and that's all that matters. If you ever find yourself in a similar situation, don't ever feel that you must live a certain way. Whether in your own home, someone else's, or an entirely new space, it's your life, choice, comfort zone, and boundaries.

What makes your living space comfortable for you?

Fifteen

GETTING BACK TO WORK

After my husband passed away, I took two weeks off from work. Upon returning, my therapist recommended I have one of my co-workers proofread my work, at least for the first couple of weeks anyway, because when we experience catastrophic events like sudden traumatic loss, it can be difficult to focus. My position required a high level of accuracy and attention to detail. I felt terrible creating additional work for my co-workers, but I also felt better knowing that there would be less of a chance that I would make potentially costly mistakes.

Fortunately, I had a boss and co-workers who supported me and could empathize with my situation. From sessions with my therapist to meetings with my real estate agent, business broker, and attorney, to appointments with my doctor and physical therapist, and working through the criminal case (the list goes on), my therapist equated this time to working three full-time jobs; believe me, it felt like it. I took a lot of time off, and accommodations were made due to my absences. I am sure there were times when it strained things, yet they handled it so well, and I will always be grateful for that.

About a year and a half after returning to work, most of the major processes I had to deal with were complete, and I decided it was time for a real break, so I quit my job to take a short sabbatical. It was not an easy decision to make. It was scary. Even though I had only been working for the company for about three years, I had progressed to a key managerial role and wore multiple hats. As with filling any position, I was well aware of the burden this might place on my colleagues and the process involved in finding someone to replace me.

But here's the thing, I was broken. I was tired. I was mentally burned out. For me, I had to consider what was more important. My job or my health and my mental and physical sanity. I knew that it was critical to my healing and well-being. I felt like I would break if I didn't take the time to care for myself. It may not be an option for everyone, and I do not take the opportunity I had for granted. It would not have been possible if my husband and I had not had life insurance. If my situation had been different, I would have researched other ways to make it happen because it was that important for me and my sanity. After a few short months, I was ready to work again and in a much stronger and more positive place. My contribution as an employee to a company would be that much better.

List three things your co-workers can do to respect your journey with grief.

Sixteen

HIS PRESENCE

One month after Jack passed, I received a document-sized envelope from an organization that deals with organ and tissue donation. I wasn't expecting anything from them and wondered what it could be. I carefully opened the envelope to find a certificate inside along with a letter to notify me that his corneas had helped restore sight for that of a twenty-eight-year-old woman. It was an incredible moment.

I had experienced firsthand how it can make a difference in the life of another human being, and I can only imagine the gift that it was to this young woman. I called Jack's mom and sister to let them know, and then I called his office and had one of the employees put me on speakerphone to let his entire crew know. They appreciated hearing about it, and it also comforted them.

It was one of the more joyful moments among many upsetting and stressful ones. It was a miracle that meant my late husband was still making a difference in this world, even beyond his life.

Around that same time, I had an appointment at the cemetery to arrange for Jack's remains to be laid to rest. It was the first time I had been to this cemetery, and I was unfamiliar with the area, so before I left, I plugged the address into the navigation system in my car.

One of the things that he complained about whenever he rode in my car was that I had the voice for the navigation system turned off. I did this because the sound of the voice annoyed me. He would ask me how I could get anywhere without the voice giving me the instructions, and I told him I would glance at the screen, which continually frustrated him.

On my way to the cemetery, I was very close but needed to figure out where to turn as I had hit an area with an unidentified road. Right then, the navigation system's voice came on and directed me to the next turn. Specific settings had to be changed for the voice to be turned on or off, and it had seemingly turned on all by itself. I had not changed the settings to turn the voice back on. I rolled my eyes, looked up with a smirk, and said, "Really, Jack? Really?" There was no question in my mind that it was him helping me get to the cemetery. That was the only time the navigation voice came on in my car and never returned. He was there to help me when I needed him, just like he had all our lives.

Seventeen

THAT'S HIS BUSINESS

Jack had owned his business for almost twelve years when he died. I did not have much direct contact with his employees after he passed away, and it wasn't for any other reason except that it was just very difficult for me. Since the incident had taken place at his work, it made it impossible for me to go back there again after it happened.

Even the tiniest thought of it gave me extreme anxiety, and to this day, I still have difficulty driving anywhere near the building without those feelings resurfacing. I have also never requested a copy of nor read the police report, and I have no interest in doing so. I was "there" on the phone with him when it happened. I was a witness. And that is more than I ever needed to know.

Unfortunately, there were times when other people who did know more details would share them in front of me without giving any consideration as to whether or not I wanted to hear them, which created unwanted mental imagery that I have since worked hard to try and erase from my mind.

One of the worst visual imaginations came when I received a call from the insurance company handling all the policies for Jack's company. They contacted me to provide instructions on submitting the invoice to receive reimbursement for the bio-hazard cleanup of my late husband's office. For those who might not be familiar with this, bio-hazard cleanup is the process of cleaning, sanitizing, and deodorizing an area after a crime, sudden death, or accident has occurred, including blood and other bodily fluids. I reviewed the invoice before submitting it and found that it listed everything that had been cleaned up in detail. After submitting it, I folded it up, filed it away, and never looked at it again.

One of Jack's family members had assisted in setting this service up right after the police investigation was complete. Getting operations back up and running as quickly as possible was crucial. I had to think about employees with jobs and families to worry about. Pending work and orders came to a complete halt for a few days, so we needed to get back on track as quickly as possible to keep the business running.

To this day, I don't know how his employees could ever go back to work after what had happened. Not to mention members of his family who helped sort and organize paperwork right after it happened and continued working in the office to help keep things running until the business was sold. I cannot imagine how difficult it must have been for them, and I commend them for having the strength and ability to do so. I repeatedly learned throughout this process that we don't know how strong we are until we have to be, and Jack's employees and family members were a true testament to that.

I completely understand that some people feel or believe they need to revisit a place of tragedy to provide them with closure, and I don't discount that at all. I completely empathize with that. Everyone needs to do what works for them, no matter what others think they should do. As often as I had to be strong and do things that I didn't want to do, some things were just too difficult for me, and it was my business to decide what those were and how I would handle them. Those were my boundaries. I prefer to remember places and people in their times of happiness and not in sorrow. In the case of my late husband's employees, I feel so bad they didn't have a choice unless they wanted to find work elsewhere. We needed to keep the business running without further interruption, and moving it to another location would have been an enormous undertaking.

Some of Jack's employees were new since the last time I had been to his office, so I had never even met them, but I tried to take care of them in ways that I knew my husband would have. Occasionally, I would have lunch ordered and delivered to them. Once, it was pizzas; the next time, it was boxed lunches. I had no experience with my husband's business and had no idea how to run it. Not to mention, I was working a full-time job and didn't have the time for both. I was fortunate to have some of his family members who could help run the business until things could get sorted out. Without their help, I would not have been able to keep the doors open.

A couple of months after the business was back up and running again, I hired a business broker to help start the process of selling it. As previously mentioned, I had no idea how to run it, which added stress and emotional turmoil that I did not want. Business brokers are basically like having a real estate agent for a business, except that, at least in my experience, it felt like it required a lot more work throughout the entire process for all parties involved, and it does not stop until the day you sign on the dotted line. There are constant requests for extensive records and reports. If you own or have ever owned a business, you can only imagine the process of transferring licenses, permits, accounts, property, etc. I won't bore you with the details here, but the process took about eight months in my case, and the business sale was complete by the end of the year. I met the new owner when we signed the final documents. That day was fraught with mixed emotions.

Jack put everything he had into his business, working 12-hour days, six days a week most weeks. He barely took time off and never stayed home unless he was very sick, which was not often at all. He had his hands on every single part of the business. I know in my heart, without a doubt, that my late husband would not have wanted me to try and run the business myself and that I had made the best decision. On the day that the official change of hands was to take place, I still did not feel comfortable going to my husband's office. Still, after speaking with my business broker about my not being physically present, we agreed that it would be good for me to be present somehow.

I opted to call in and have him put me on speakerphone while we met to let the employees know I had sold the business. I thanked them for hanging in there when I knew they had all endured and were continuing to face some very challenging days and months ahead. It was a very bittersweet moment for me because I knew that my husband had put so much hard work, time, and effort into building his business, but I was also relieved that there was one less thing, one huge thing, to worry about.

Eighteen

SO SORRY FOR YOUR LOSS

The first sympathy card I received right after Jack passed away was a large, trifold card from the hair salon he had been going to for over twenty years. It was filled with handwritten messages from every single employee. I was touched by this more than I could ever express. Our families were so thankful for the multiple floral arrangements, stacks of sympathy cards, and donations made in Jack's name to the local YMCA, where he played sports as a young boy. But what was most comforting for me were the messages from people who wanted to share stories about my late husband, especially those I did not know.

If you ever feel hesitant to send a card, write an email, or even share a story with someone who has lost a loved one, please don't be. You may have an anecdote or memory to share that could be comforting. It might be difficult for them to read at first, and they may not even read it right away, but it can also be a blessing to have them to look back on and read, even years later.

Some of the saddest moments I had to endure were when I would run into someone I hadn't seen in a while who didn't know Jack had passed away. I would be greeted with this big smile, sometimes a hug, a "How are you?" and then, "How's Jack?" Those were the toughest. When I thought everyone knew, there would be one person who didn't, and I received all kinds of reactions when this happened.

One morning, I went into the Starbucks that Jack used to go to near our home every day on his way to work. I hadn't been there for about a month as it took me some time to revisit places he and I had been together. But I finally felt like I could walk through the doors again, and his favorite barista happened to be working that day. She greeted me with her usual smiling self and asked me where Jack was because she hadn't seen him in a while. I motioned for her to walk down to the end of the counter so I could speak with her privately and let her know that he had passed away. She immediately broke down into tears and ran to the back of the store. I was so heartbroken. It was the first time I had to tell someone face-to-face that he had passed away, and it was proof that my late husband truly impacted everyone he met. The loss was felt deeply by everyone who came in contact with him.

It's one of the reasons why I stopped wearing my wedding ring shortly after Jack passed away. Not only because it was a sad reminder for me, but it also invited questions from outsiders who didn't know that he had died. It was easier for me emotionally not to have this beacon of curiosity and reminder on my ring finger that what I used to have was gone. I did, however, want my late husband's wedding ring back, which was not as easy to obtain as one would think. Since he was wearing it when he was murdered, it was evidence, so I had to wait until the internal investigation was complete before I could get it.

I had asked the victim's advocate I was working with through the prosecutor's office about this a couple of times. She sent a formal request to the detective I had been working with initially, who then had to request it from the lead detective on the case, and then he sent a request to the police chief, who could provide approval for me to retrieve my late husband's ring.

After the request was approved, I received a call from the lead detective, who arranged to meet me at a coffee shop near my office so that I could collect the ring. I didn't know who I was looking for when I arrived as we had never met. He spotted and texted me to let me know his description and where he was sitting. I walked over to him, formally introduced myself, and sat face-to-face at a small table for two right in the middle of the shop. It was pretty busy as it was mid-morning on a weekday and located in an area with many office buildings.

I quickly realized it was not the smartest choice for a meeting place since we were there to make a pretty sensitive transaction. There was a high probability that I would get emotional about the situation in a public place full of people. In light of that, even though I had a prime opportunity to ask questions, I didn't ask him too much because I wanted to protect myself from anything that might cause me additional pain. There was no sense in that for me, just as what had happened made no sense. In my mind, there will never be a reason for what happened, and there were some things that I didn't want to know. But we did chat a bit about his part in the investigation and his long road trip with Bill when he was transferred back from the state he fled to. When we were finished chatting, it was time for me to get Jack's ring.

A manila envelope with a slight bump was lying on the table between the detective and myself. He had me open the envelope to confirm that it was my late husband's ring. Inside the envelope was a clear police evidence zippered polybag with the case number written on it and a description of the contents. The location where the "evidence" was found read, "Left hand, ring finger." I started crying the second I pulled the ring out of the bag.

I tried to keep my tears as under control as possible, but fighting it wasn't easy. It was something Jack was wearing when he died. I had put that ring on his finger on our wedding day. I hastily put the ring back in the bag, and the detective asked me to sign a "Release of Evidence" form. We chatted a bit longer, and then I had to return to work. When I returned to my roommate's house that night, I tucked the envelope with the bag and ring in my sock drawer. I didn't look at it again for a while. Later, I received a silver chain as a gift from my roommate, to which I added his ring so I could wear them around my neck from time to time.

I know I am not the only one who suffered a loss here. Our families, our friends, our neighbors, his employees, his clients, his hairdresser, and his favorite barista; the list continues. They all suffered a loss, and I feel for each and every single one of them. I have often thought that if I had the strength to stand up and speak at the memorial service, I would have said, "I am sorry for your loss, and I am so deeply sorry." I cannot imagine how anyone must have felt or what they must have been going through when this sudden tragedy occurred. We were all dealing with a tremendous loss. It was not just my loss but a loss for so many others.

Nineteen

OUR 10TH ANNIVERSARY

Our 10th wedding anniversary was about seven weeks after Jack passed away. In honor of the day, I had taken a day off work and spent some time early in the day getting our house ready to sell. Most of the packing had already been done, thanks to several wonderful friends who generously donated their time to help me. I kept myself busy that day by running errands and meeting a friend for lunch. I wasn't sure if I wanted to celebrate, but the couple I was living with had offered to take me out to dinner that night, and I decided it would be a good thing for me to do. We ended up going to one of the restaurants that my husband and I used to frequent, which at the time, I thought would be a lovely way to honor him and the things we used to do. Honestly, while it was a beautiful evening out with my friends, it wasn't the same, and I haven't returned to that restaurant since.

I received a couple of phone calls and text messages from family and friends that day with wishes of support, but overall, the day came and went lackluster. Part of the reason it was difficult for me was that we had planned to take a special trip for our anniversary that we had been looking forward to that didn't happen, and this was a reminder of that.

One of the most challenging parts of the packing process was going through Jack's belongings. I don't remember when I decided to do it, but I remember doing it alone. For whatever reason, it wasn't something I wanted help with. I went through all his clothing, piece by piece, setting aside his favorite shirts and hats and a few other random items, such as framed photos and a watch I had given him. I packed everything else into boxes or bags and drove them to a donation center. I neatly placed the clothing and other items I had chosen to save in a plastic bin and closed the lid.

This process reminded me of a flashback from just a few days after Jack died. One of his family members offered to take his truck from his office and park it at their house until I could figure out what to do with it. I didn't have the strength to go and get it myself. I didn't even want to see it. It was too painful for me. Before the truck was moved, Jack's mom removed all of his personal belongings and placed them in an open cardboard tray, like the ones you get at big box/warehouse stores, and dropped it off at my sister's house, where I was staying at that time.

That was the first time I had seen anything that had belonged to him since he'd passed away just a few days before. It was very emotional for both me and my sister.

I learned a valuable lesson that day that, since then, I have shared with others. And that is that if you are in a position where someone asks if you can help retrieve the personal items of someone who has passed away, I suggest putting them in a box or bag that you can close and cannot see through. That way, the recipient can decide when they are ready to go through them. For some people, this may not be an issue. It wasn't for Jack's mom. But for others, it can be an emotionally devastating and shocking experience. There is no way to know how anyone will react to seeing items their lost loved one once owned. Grieving someone after a loss can be enough, so anything that can be done to help shield them from the trigger of more pain will be appreciated.

One of the questions I have been asked a few times is why I couldn't live in our home again. Honestly, the house didn't feel like a "home" to me anymore. Everywhere I turned, there were just too many reminders and memories that made me feel sad. We had built a life together there for over ten years. We had hosted several family gatherings, from birthdays and graduations to holidays, dinners with friends, an engagement party, and a baby shower. But mostly, it was the place we came home to every night, and it was just not the same without him there. I would not have been able to be in the kitchen without wishing he would come through the door, sit at the island, and go through the mail while I cooked dinner. I would miss the nights we would sit in the TV room, order takeout, and watch a movie. I would not have been able to sleep alone in that big house. I knew these were all things I didn't have the strength to deal with.

Not to mention, I would not have been able to handle the financial burden and upkeep of a 3,000-square-foot house on my own. As if dealing with all the other things I had to deal with in the wake of Jack's passing wasn't enough, I endured some significant setbacks while selling the home. There were not one but two bad inspections. The first cost me the loss of the first sale, and the second forced me to break down into uncontrollable tears at my desk while at work. Both cost a lot of time and money. (Again, I stress the importance of life insurance.) I joke that our seventeen-year-old home was practically new when all was said and done. Going through that helped seal the deal for me, knowing I had made the right decision. On December 23rd, I turned off all the lights and locked the doors for the last time. I only returned a couple of times after that to pick up straggling mail from the new owners.

As I've mentioned, I know everyone deals with grief differently, and I completely understand and respect that it might be comforting for some people to stay in your home. Just because it didn't work for me doesn't mean it would not work for someone else. I am here to share my stories in the hopes that if there is anyone out there who did have the same experience, they will know that they are not alone. This decision was about eliminating as much as possible from my life that would cause pain, stress, and burden.

Twenty

THE CRIMINAL CASE

Never in a million years did I think I would be involved in a criminal case. Let alone one involving a murder. One of the scariest situations I faced was when I had to go to the courthouse to meet with the prosecuting attorney and victim's advocate assigned to my case. I was given a choice of going to the courthouse downtown or one located just south of the city. If I chose to go to the courthouse downtown, it would mean that I would be in the same building where Bill was currently incarcerated. Once I knew that my decision was simple. I would be heading to the location south of the city. I wanted to keep as far away from him as humanly possible. Just the thought of even knowing that he was there gave me anxiety.

I remember going to work that morning and barely being able to concentrate. When it was time to go to the courthouse, I was shaking and could feel my heart pounding as I drove, feeling more nervous as I got closer, knowing that soon I would meet the people who would help put Bill behind bars, hopefully for life.

I walked into the courthouse, through security, and to the suite number I had been given. I let the receptionist know who I was, took a seat, and waited. A pleasant woman came out to greet me, who turned out to be my victim's advocate. Even though we were still very early on in the process, she had been such a help to me already. She helped explain the process of the criminal investigation and legal proceedings and was there to answer any questions for me. She walked me back to a small room where we met the prosecuting attorney. We sat down, and I remember him saying he felt terrible that we had to meet in this "interrogation room" because it was a busy day at the courthouse, so they had limited space. The first thing I did was cry, and my voice quivered as tears ran down my face. I could barely squeak out in a whisper, "This is so scary."

They allowed me to take a minute to compose myself and then began the questioning. The purpose of our meeting wasn't to discuss the incident itself but for me to share with them who Jack was as a person. They wanted to get to know him better. He was not just the victim of a crime. He was a human being.

I spoke about our relationship, his sense of humor, and his character. Soon, I felt more relaxed and even laughed at one point as I shared anecdotes about him. I spoke about how I would wake up to Jack singing in the shower, usually songs by Elvis. His dad loved Elvis and could sing the words to virtually any of his songs on cue. He was a living Elvis jukebox, if you will. So, some of that had naturally rubbed off on Jack. He loved music in general (and constantly messed up song lyrics). He loved fast food and was known for giving directions based on where fast-food restaurants were located (e.g., "Take a left at the McDonalds and then a right at the Taco Bell. If you've passed Burger King you've gone too far.") He loved going to the movies and wine tasting. But most of all, he just loved to chill out at home in his "man cave" (a.k.a. The upstairs bonus room in our house).

After sharing stories about Jack, I had an opportunity to ask any questions I had. As I had experienced when I spoke with the detective, I was cautious, fearing it might conjure unwanted visions or memories. But one question I had was how the prison sentence length and maximum length would be determined. The prosecuting attorney showed me a chart to equate the sentence by matching the number of murders committed with the number of victims murdered. In this case, it was one murder and one victim. The maximum prison sentence for a first-time murder of one person was twenty-six and a half years.

Take a moment to swallow that.

I thought that number was an absolute joke when I first heard it. Even though, in this case, it meant that Bill would be in prison for the rest of his life (He would be nearing one hundred years old if he were to live until his release date.), it didn't seem like nearly enough time considering he had committed murder. What I couldn't get out of my mind was other people going through similar situations, but where the perpetrator was much younger. What if someone were to commit a similar crime but was only twenty years old? What happens when they get out of prison at forty-six years old?

I couldn't imagine facing that reality or the fear I would feel knowing that someone who committed such a horrible crime could be released. In my case, the prosecutor would also ask for a gun enhancement, adding another five years to the sentence, still making the total sentence only thirty-one and a half years. I have been asked many times about the death penalty, and if that had been an option, I would have wanted that to be the sentence. Honestly, I never know how to answer that. It's a very complicated and delicate question. For the sake of sharing the information, I discovered that a little over a year before my husband's murder, a moratorium was placed on the death penalty in our state, and a little over three years later, the death penalty was abolished.

Despite the terrible anxiety I had experienced leading up to this meeting and the sensitive nature of some of our discussions, I felt better after meeting face-to-face with the team working to put Jack's murderer behind bars. It was comforting for me to put faces to their names. It was only the beginning of a process that would go on for several months. With each scheduled hearing, I would receive a call with an update, and each time it would be postponed, there wouldn't be enough information to conduct the hearing, or the defense would request more time. I thought there was a light at the end of the tunnel when we thought the defense was willing to accept a plea bargain, and I thought it would be over, but then, a short time later, the defense backed out. It was devastating. I felt like they were playing a hurtful game. At this point, there was no way of telling how long it would take. It could take months or even years before it was over. So, I just had to wait and hope it would be over soon.

Twenty One

SHARING MEMORIES

As previously mentioned, Jack was a huge golf fan and liked to get out and play whenever possible. We had attended a couple of professional golf tournaments together, but when we heard that the *U.S. Open* was coming to our area, he was so excited and just had to go. He was always giving to others and rarely did anything for himself. So, when the opportunity to go to this tournament arose, it was time for him to treat himself. He bought the best tickets he could buy and was so looking forward to it. He had purchased the tickets over a year in advance, and the tournament was less than three months after he passed away. I knew that my husband would not have wanted me to miss the tournament just because he wasn't there with me. He would have wanted me to enjoy it. So, I asked one of our dearest and closest friends to go with me, and we had a fabulous time. Ultimately, I was sad that Jack didn't get to attend, but I was so glad we decided to go in his honor.

She was one of Jack's closest friends and was the one who introduced us. She had been telling me for months about this guy she wanted to set me up with, and I had been reluctant for quite some time because when she first mentioned it, I had just gotten out of a long-term relationship and had decided to take a break from dating. Finally, one afternoon, I agreed to meet him. She suggested we go on a group date with him and his best friend.

Little did I know that he would end up being my future husband. We met at a restaurant, and I remember seeing him walk through the door and my friend pointing him out to me, and I just "knew." That was it for me. We were engaged six months later and married the following year.

The three of us are still very dear friends, and I find comfort in knowing we have a shared history with Jack. It's a special bond that connects us and many others. I feel so blessed to have friendships that have continued beyond the loss and that we can lean on each other when needed. I have found, especially right after it happened, that people may have found it difficult to talk to me about Jack for fear of how it would affect me. But for the most part, I was open to hearing stories about him, especially if they asked if it was okay to share them first. Photos are difficult for me, and I still have trouble looking at them. When I was in group therapy, which I will discuss in more detail later in this book, there was a session where we were all asked to bring photos of our lost loved one. I only brought a handful, whereas others in the group brought many. But that's what I was comfortable with, and that's okay. If you're not comfortable hearing stories or looking at photos of your lost loved one, set those boundaries. They are yours to set and no one else's.

Some people might be scared to speak with you about your loss or even approach you. If you're comfortable with it, break the ice for them. Be the one to welcome the conversation. It has been my experience that they will be relieved that you did. It's essential to have and keep those connections with people. It is also an excellent reminder of how important it is to share your stories with your friends and family, as it allows them to be remembered and retold from person to person for years to come.

Twenty Two

GETTING AWAY FROM IT ALL

About three months after Jack passed away, I took my first vacation. One of my best girlfriends and I had planned this trip for months, and I didn't want to cancel it. I was relieved I had something to look forward to and escape from what I was dealing with. Part of me wanted to take the trip to escape everything I had going on. But part of me also felt a little bit guilty. Should I be going on a vacation just months after my husband passed? Should I be having fun? Shouldn't I be grieving? Taking a break from things and having fun made me feel self-conscious. It made me feel as though people might be judging me or that they would think that I was over the loss of Jack and was moving on with my life. But that was not the case. I think breaks are necessary. You must take time out for yourself and do things that make you happy. It is essential to your survival and crucial to the healing process. I just needed a break and a change of scenery. I needed to go somewhere where everywhere I went didn't remind me of my late husband. I don't think that you should let anyone judge you for how you work through tragedy. This vacation was my time to put everything out of my mind, even if it was just for a few days.

I will never forget the relaxation I felt when I walked into our hotel room and saw a patio with a beautiful view of the beach, ocean, and palm trees. A hotel associate brought our bags to the room and offered complimentary welcome cocktails. Life, at that moment, was good. For the next four days, everything was carefree and fun. There was no schedule: phone calls, meetings, expectations, deadlines, or pressure. I don't think I even used my phone other than to snap a few photos. It was just what the doctor ordered, and I knew I had done the right thing.

Before I knew it, it was coming up on the 4th of July, and my roommate and I had a four-day weekend ahead of us, so we decided to take a spontaneous road trip to a local resort town. Usually, you need to book a year in advance to find a place to stay on a holiday weekend, but as luck would have it, we were able to find the last available room in a little bed & breakfast. We went wine tasting, watched a beautiful fireworks show, spent some lazy time by the lake, ate delicious meals, and laughed (think junior high slumber party). I had not laughed that hard in months, and I needed it.

I continued to take weekend trips every few months, each time trying not to let myself feel bad for wanting to take care of myself and have some fun. I chose to honor my choices and decisions because they were what I felt was best for me and what I wanted. Just as I had discussed when I was talking about self-care, you have to take time out for yourself and do whatever makes you happy. For me, it was essential to my survival and crucial to the healing process.

Name one place you'd like to visit and write down one thing you can do to make it happen.

Twenty Three

ANNIVERSARIES AND HIS BIRTHDAY

A couple more months passed, and it was the 11th anniversary of the day that we got engaged. My roommate texted me that day and asked if I wanted to do anything to honor the day, and at first, I wasn't sure.

I thought about the day that Jack proposed. We were on a weekend getaway on the Oregon Coast, and after we arrived and got settled in, he took me for a drive along Highway 101. We stopped at several lighthouses and lookout points along the way. He and I had gone ring shopping a couple of weeks prior, so whenever we stopped, I started to get suspicious and thought that maybe he would propose, but he didn't. Then, that evening, we had dinner reservations at our favorite waterfront restaurant. The waiter sat us at a perfect table looking right out at the ocean, and I thought to myself, "This is it!"

Then I started to think that maybe Jack wouldn't propose that weekend. Perhaps it would be too obvious. Once we finished dinner, the waiter asked if we wanted dessert, and Jack asked if we could get something to go because he wanted to take a walk on the beach at sunset. We got back to the hotel, changed our clothes, and he grabbed a blanket to take with us down to the beach. Jack accidentally dropped the blanket as we walked onto the sand, and I heard a clinking sound. It was at that moment that he proposed. I remember a group of college kids having a fire on the beach, and they were all clapping and cheering when Jack put the ring on my finger. He opened the blanket to reveal a bottle of champagne and two glasses, which thankfully did not break when he dropped them. We celebrated with a glass of champagne at sunset.

I decided that I wanted to relive that moment. My roommate and I went to this little neighborhood wine bar, and since we didn't have a view of the sunset, we looked up what time sunset would be so we could toast at that time. The bartender poured us two glasses of champagne, and we waited a few minutes until it was time. There was music playing overhead from a satellite radio station, and the moment we clinked our glasses, my husband's favorite song, "Somewhere Over the Rainbow" by Israel Kamakawiwo'ole, started to play over the speakers. We looked at each other in shock! It was unbelievable that song would come on at that moment as it's not a song that plays very often. My roommate and I looked at each other and knew Jack was there with us. There was no doubt in my mind that I was exactly where I was supposed to be.

Just a couple of weeks later, I celebrated what would have been Jack's 43rd birthday. I did not want this to be a sad day, and knew I wanted to honor him somehow. He was a huge football fan, and there happened to be a pre-season game on TV that night. It was a weeknight, and if he was alive, I knew that all he would have wanted to do was hang out at home, watch the game, and eat pizza. So, we rounded up a couple of people, got into our football gear, ordered pizza, and watched the game. It was the most fun evening, and I knew that this impromptu pizza party was the perfect way to honor him on this special day by doing something he would have loved to do.

Every year, a local golf tournament occurred right around Jack's birthday, and it became a tradition to go as part of his birthday celebration. He looked forward to going every year. I decided I wanted to be there and even managed to recruit friends to accompany me. It wasn't anything that significantly impacted me emotionally. Still, it was something that he loved to do every year, so it would be fun to participate. It was all part of continuing to honor him and the person he was and enjoying the things he loved to do. I know he would be so happy that I was getting out and doing these things even though he was not there to do them with me.

Honoring a lost loved one is very personal and individual for everyone. While I honored my feelings of sadness and allowed myself to grieve, I also found happiness in doing things that Jack loved to do. In many ways, reliving the good times we had spent together was fun, and I was lucky enough to have some willing participants join me. But everyone has a right to honor those they have lost however they choose, and I wish everyone much peace and comfort as you journey through remembering your loved one.

Twenty Four

THE "FIRSTS"

One of the inevitable truths about losing someone is that there will always be "firsts" that we must endure. In my experience, many occurred within the first few days and weeks after Jack passed away. Like the first morning, I would not kiss him goodbye, or the first evening, I would not hug him when he walked in the door. The first Saturday morning he would not bring me coffee, and when I realized that we would never have another date night. The first family gathering, he would not be sitting with us at the dinner table.

The first time that I met up with our friends by myself and the first time I would venture to the Oregon Coast alone. The first time I shopped at the grocery store as a "single" and my first road trip on my own. The first time I heard a song on the radio that I knew he loved. All the firsts that he has missed with our nieces and nephews. "Firsts" can come out of nowhere and bring all kinds of emotions to the surface, and they are different for everyone as they pertain to the unique experiences you had with your loved one. They can be a happy, bittersweet, scary, or sad reminder of your loss.

Jack helped me to become a much stronger person than I was before. Whenever I was nervous or scared about something, he would be the one to deliver a pep talk and give me support and confidence. In some ways, I have always carried that with me. As I have said before, you don't know how strong you are until you have to be, and throughout this process, I have most certainly had to be strong. I told myself that I had to be strong because, in my mind, I didn't have a choice. Being strong was my only option. As the saying goes, you either get bitter or better. I chose to get better.

Twenty Five

THE HOLIDAYS

Christmas is my favorite holiday, and while Jack was not quite as into it as I was, my love for it rubbed off on him more and more each year. He even watched *Hallmark* holiday movies with me (he was into them more than he'd like to admit). He was thrilled that I never asked him to help me with decorations, and I didn't mind because I enjoy doing it. I would pull out all the decorations the day after Thanksgiving every year and spend the entire day putting them up. But the year Jack passed away was the first year I would not be decorating our home in ten years, and the first year I would not be Christmas shopping for him. So, I chose to enjoy as many holiday experiences with my family and friends as possible and not get all wrapped up in the stress and craziness that can come with that time of year.

It was the first Christmas for our great-niece, so I went with my niece and her husband to get her picture taken with Santa. Then we went to a local annual holiday performance, and I spent the night at their house on Christmas Eve to be with them on Christmas morning. I could not have asked for a better way to spend the holiday. My niece and her husband even filled up a stocking for me. The next day, I was invited to have Christmas with my roommate's family, and it was a wonderful evening. I knew Jack would be happy I was still participating in the holidays and not letting it pass me by.

I went to a friend's house for a New Year's Eve party a few days later. For many, the New Year brings the opportunity for new beginnings and the turning of a page, but for me, this was not my New Year. My New Year would begin once I had made it through a year without Jack. For me, this night was just an opportunity to relax and have some fun with my friends. I observed as everyone else celebrated the start of their New Year while I still had about three more months to go before I would celebrate mine.

Twenty Six

CATHARTIC RELEASE

About nine months passed, and I was referred to a therapy group offered through grief services at a nearby hospital. It is specific to helping people like myself who have lost someone to a sudden and tragic death, such as an accident, murder, or suicide. I had never taken part in group therapy before, and I cannot tell you how much it helped and has continued to help me. The process started with an individual, face-to-face meeting with one of the therapist facilitators of the group so that she could hear my story and get an idea of where I was in my grief process. Everyone in the group had their unique situation and was on their own timeline. Then, the group meetings took place for ten weeks, and each week had a different topic, lesson, and exercise. The group I was in had three members, and both of the other members had experienced loss through suicide.

For several months after Jack passed away, there were many times when I felt like I was on the outside looking in on this surreal life. It was like I was hovering above myself. I felt like everyone I passed on the street looked at me like I was an alien, even though I knew they had no idea what was happening inside of me. Being a part of this group was such a blessing for me because even though we had a completely different story to tell, we could still relate to each other on some level because of what we were all going through. We connected differently than people who have not experienced anything like this. While it was mentally and physically exhausting and probably one of the most emotionally grueling things I have ever gone through, it was so beneficial. I am genuinely thankful that I was able to take part. I have remained in contact with the group members, and while we don't connect often, I find it so comforting to have that connection. About a year after completing the group therapy sessions, I was asked by one of the therapists if we could have a follow-up session to discuss how I was doing. It was video recorded and used as an internal training tool for future program facilitators.

This program was so vital to me and had helped me in so many ways that it was the least I could do to give back in some small way. I have also shared my story as part of the *Hey Human Podcast by Susan Ruth* (Episode 34—Diane: Through The Eyes Of Love). In recent years, I participated in a panel discussion on gun violence and virtual group discussions on grief during the pandemic, attended worldwide by those who have experienced a sudden, tragic loss.

While I can't say that my participation in any of these was easy, I can say that, over time, it has made it somewhat easier for me to share my story with others. It can be extremely difficult to speak to anyone about it, and while I would hope that people would not judge me, I think that part of the reason why there were times that I felt that I did not want to share my story is because I feared judgment. What will people think of me when I tell them I'm a widow because my husband was murdered by his uncle? Will they feel that he did something to deserve this? What will they think of me associating with someone with a family member who would do something like that? Not everyone will accept, comprehend, or understand the information in the same way, but in the end, it's my story to tell, and I can share it whenever and with whomever I choose.

Twenty Seven

"HOLIDAYS"

I told Jack I didn't believe in Valentine's Day when we first met. I don't have anything against anyone who wants to celebrate it. You do you! I just don't feel that there should be a specific date on the calendar that places unnecessary pressure on people to find ways to express their love to their significant other. It should be spontaneous and whenever it feels right for you. I wanted Jack to avoid going out and spending money on flowers that were three times the price that day or buying chocolates, perfume, or anything like that. The only thing I like about Valentine's Day is the half-price chocolate the next day. When the first Valentine's Day rolled around, even though I had vetoed tradition, I only requested that I not have to cook dinner that night.

Jack could not cook (at all) and told me a story about how he used several pots and pans the first time he tried to make boxed macaroni and cheese. He burnt the water to the bottom of the pot and didn't realize that you needed milk and butter to make it. When I went to his house for the first time, he had a case of beer and some old leftover chili in the fridge, and that was it. If I didn't cook dinner, it usually meant that we would be going out. So, we went out for pizza for our first Valentine's Day together. It became our annual tradition, and when the first Valentine's Day arrived after he passed away, one of my friends and I went out for pizza, and that was the last time I did that.

The last "first" before the one-year anniversary of Jack's passing was the anniversary of our first date. When Jack and I arranged our first date, neither of us realized it was St. Patrick's Day, but we didn't want to go to an Irish bar either. So we went to a Mexican restaurant instead, which was almost completely empty. Each year, we made a point to go anywhere but an Irish bar on St. Patrick's Day. So when my roommates asked where I wanted to go that day, we decided to go to a small local restaurant for happy hour. It was a nice, quiet evening, and after dinner, I relaxed at home just as I would have had he been there. I would not have wanted to spend that day any other way.

Twenty Eight

ONE YEAR LATER

As the first anniversary of Jack's death approached, I knew that the one thing I did not want to do was make it a sad day. I wanted to honor him. I wanted to celebrate his life while he was on this earth and not make it about the tragedy of his death. Allowing that day to affect me negatively would mean that it had gotten the best of me, that Bill had gotten the best of me, and I was not going to let that happen. I decided to take a weekend trip with one of my dear girlfriends to the Oregon Coast.

It was a short trip, but we spent the weekend doing everything my husband and I would have done if we had gone there. We had lunch at a seaside town, made keepsakes at a glassblowing studio, ate at our favorite restaurant, played slots at the casino, and drank wine. When we returned from our weekend at the beach, I remember thinking, "This is *my* New Year. I can finally turn a page and start again."

Twenty Nine

THE SENTENCING

The sentencing took place about fifteen months after Jack was murdered. My victim's advocate contacted me to see if anyone who knew him would like to write a Victim Impact Statement, a letter of character on his behalf, which the judge would read before the sentencing. In addition to the one I wrote, the judge received several of them from family members and friends of Jack's.

Writing a Victim Impact Statement

Writing a Victim Impact Statement will not only explain to a judge the impact of the crime on you and those they knew, but it will also bring a human voice to a lost loved one and help the judge better understand who they were as a person. Visit this link to learn more:

Victim Support Services—Victim Impact Statements[18]

Since I chose not to be at the courthouse, I prepared an additional statement to be shared with the judge that his sister read for me. In my statement, I shared a story about how I was preparing to host about 20 people for Christmas Eve dinner at our house. It was the 23rd, and I had gotten off work early that day and had rushed home to start the preparations. Jack knew I would not want to cook dinner for us that night as I was preparing food for the following day, so he called me and said he would pick up some takeout for us on his way home.

Quite a few people had the same idea because when my husband arrived at the restaurant, he was approached by a frantic waiter who told him he would have to wait a bit longer for our order. She offered him a free soda, and he told her he would run to the bank machine and return in a few minutes. He noticed this poor girl was working alone and trying to keep up as best she could, but other customers were getting frustrated and angry with her. He knew it wasn't her fault that there was a high volume of orders and insufficient staff.

When he returned, she approached his truck and handed him our order and the credit card slip, and he gave her a cash

[18]www.victimsupportservices.org/help-for-victims/victim-impact-statements

tip in the same amount as the order total. He said, “Merry Christmas!” She smiled at him as her eyes began to well with tears as she replied with deep appreciation, “Thank you so much.” I will never forget him sharing that story with me when he got home. Just as so many angels came to my rescue through this process, I feel that that night Jack was hers.

I was not present at the sentencing because I did not want to be anywhere near Bill, but a few of Jack’s family members and friends attended. It just wasn’t going to work for me. I had thought about staying home that day, but the sentencing was in the afternoon, and I didn’t want to be alone at my roommate’s house all day trying to come up with distractions. I knew my mind would be racing and would have gone stir-crazy. Even though I wasn’t entirely focused that day, at least I had things to do at work. It would have been advantageous if I could be at the sentencing so the judge could see and hear from me since I was the widow and the only witness. But I told the victim’s advocate that if I were to attend, there’d better be paramedics and an ambulance ready for me because I would have a heart attack if I had to stand within 300 yards of Bill. Thankfully, it was not mandatory, so instead, she called me as soon as it was over to let me know how everything went.

Bill received the maximum sentence of twenty-six and a half years.

I don’t know how to describe how I felt at that moment. You would think it would bring some relief or maybe even an odd sense of accomplishment or happiness, but instead, I felt a massive release because I knew a significant chapter had finally been closed. I knew that Bill would be behind bars for good.

I have been asked if I would ever have wanted to talk to Bill. Ask him why he did what he did. I've clarified that I never wanted to see or be around him. Honestly, even if I were to have asked him, "Why did you do it?" it would not matter to me what his response was because there is absolutely no reason for him to have done what he did. None. He could give me a million reasons, but none of them would be valid in my mind. There is no reason. I'm sure some people won't understand this way of thinking because we are naturally conditioned to want to get answers and find out the "Why?" We struggle with these gaping holes and questions in our minds that we want to compartmentalize and organize to make sense of what happened, especially when it's this tragic. For that reason, I struggle with responding when I am asked, "Why did he do it?" because there is no reason for me.

Bill passed away in jail just five years into his sentence. I was sitting at my desk working when Jack's sister called. She and I don't talk on the phone much, let alone in the morning on a workday, so I knew something was up when I saw her number on my phone. At first, I thought maybe a family member had died or was sick. Bill was the furthest from my mind. Then she asked me if I had heard the news that Bill had died in prison. It was the same feeling I had when he was sentenced. I didn't know what to think. I guess the most relief came from knowing he would not be released from prison and could not hurt anyone else.

Thirty

LESSONS

I think I've made it pretty apparent that I have learned a lot from this experience, but one of the most important lessons that I have learned is to enjoy life more and not get caught up in the small stuff. I know that probably sounds terribly cliche, but when you've been through something as life-changing as this, many things that might have upset you before don't matter anymore. Getting upset about the little things is just a waste of time and energy. That energy can be channeled in so many more positive ways.

I have always had a positive outlook and have been thankful for what I have, but what I have gone through gave me a far more acute sense of that and reminded me of how fleeting life can be. I value experiences far more than material things.

Stuff doesn't matter to me anymore. People do. When I sold my house, I spent a lot of time purging everything I owned to the bare minimum, and I feel so much less weighed down. I would rather be out living and experiencing life than sitting in a house full of "stuff." You can't take it with you when you go, so what's the point?

I have also become more proactive and spontaneous. If there is something that I want to do and I have the means and the time to do it, I do it. Many times since I lost Jack, I have said, "Someday is today." He and I talked about so many things that we would do "someday," and guess what? "Someday" never came. So, I try not to use that word anymore. Either I do something or I don't, but I also remind myself not to feel regret. I did more in the first two years after Jack passed away than in the five years before because I truly realized how precious and short life is.

As time passed, I was asked when or if I would be ready to date again. It was about two years before I started to feel like I could be open to the possibility. But I didn't have a "timeline." I decided to go with my gut and start when I felt ready. Even when I thought I was ready, I wasn't proactively looking for a partner. Not that I would have opposed it if the opportunity had presented itself. Other people were more worried about it than I was. But it wasn't a priority for me because I didn't want to find someone just so that I wouldn't be alone for fear that I might end up settling. Life is way too short for that. If it took two or twenty years, I would want to find the right person.

It took some time before I was comfortable sharing my story with people outside my inner circle of family and friends. Sometimes, it was because I didn't feel like talking about it. Other times, it doesn't feel like the right time or person to share it with. In any situation I was in, I let my intuition be my guide. It's my story to share, not anyone else's, and I have control. My story isn't pretty, and, in some ways, I think it can be difficult for people to swallow when I tell them that I'm a widow whose husband was murdered. It has been my experience that far more people who have lost someone suddenly have been because they were ill or were in an accident, not because they were murdered. I'm sharing something that sounds unbelievable. A typical response is shock, sympathy, and confusion, followed by questions. While I've become more open to sharing these thoughts as time passes, it isn't always easy. But ultimately, I decided to share my story because I want to help others.

Everything I have shared with you in this book is based on my personal experience (or the personal experience of others who were willing to share their story). I am not a doctor, a therapist, an attorney, or any other type of certified professional, and I have not made any professional recommendations. Any decisions you make based on the content in this book are solely your own. Feel free to consider my thoughts and suggestions as you see fit.

In closing, thank you to all who have read this book. Thank you for taking the time to read my story. I do hope that if you have found anything that you can relate to, it will bring you peace in moments of grief, comfort in times of pain, strength in moments of weakness, and hope for the future in knowing that you can move forward from this and that it is possible to find happiness after tragedy. If I can get through something like this, I believe you can too.

With heartfelt compassion and endless gratitude,

Jennifer

What lessons have you learned from reading this book?

THE UNWANTED JOURNEYS OF OTHERS

Through my journey with navigating grief and loss through therapy, I met some amazing individuals who, with tremendous strength and vulnerability, agreed to share their personal experiences with sudden, traumatic loss. They opened their hearts, offering their perspectives and suggestions on how they navigated and continue to navigate their grief. Their stories remind us that grief does not discriminate and no one is alone in their journey. I hope that by sharing these additional stories of loss with you, we can find strength and healing together.

Maria's Story—Prisoner of Grief

The loss I will share is the death of a very close friend, Mahmoud, whom I met when I was traveling to Syria in 2017. Because he worked at the front desk in the hotel where I was staying, we saw each other every day and eventually became close. Even after I returned to the United States, we stayed in contact and remained close.

During the Arab Spring, I was working in Jordan with an American organization providing mental health counseling to Syrian refugees and torture survivors. At the same time, Mahmoud's older brother, who lived outside of Syria, decided to return to Syria to join the rebel army fighting the National Army. After a short time, he quickly realized what he was fighting for he did not support. He quit and returned to the country where he was living. After he left, the Syrian police came to the family home looking for him to arrest. They found, instead, Mahmoud and his younger brother, whom they arrested and confiscated their computers. Soon after, I received a Facebook message from the older brother telling me Mahmoud had been arrested and instructed me not to try to contact Mahmoud because the police would surely use this against him. Because of my work, I was well aware of the horrifying conditions and treatment Mahmoud and his brother were experiencing, and this tore me apart. It took everything I had to not replay in my mind what I imagined was happening to them. I eventually learned from a mutual friend that both Mahmoud and his younger brother died in prison and were dumped in a mass grave.

The weeks after I learned he was arrested, I was functioning superficially, at best. I had frequent nightmares and horrific thoughts that I couldn't get out of my head when I was awake. I avoided watching the news in case anything about the war came up, and at the same time, I fixated on the few pictures I had of him. I was anxious, irritable, and depressed when hearing about anyone's suffering. My tolerance for holding space for others' pain was almost non-existent. After I learned he and his brother died in prison, the images actually became less frequent because I believed neither was no longer suffering. While I had held out hope they would be released from prison, I was relieved their suffering was over, and now his family and friends could mourn them.

After Mahmoud's death, I had a difficult time supporting Syrian families who lost loved ones in the war. I found myself becoming angry and impatient when hearing these stories because Mahmoud's death was still painful. When I was at home, I often let my heart, mind, and body do what they needed to feel the full extent of my horror and sorrow. This came out of me through guttural cries, calling out to him and wailing about how sorry I was this happened to him, his brother, and his family. To get through each day, however, I had to remind myself that he was no longer in pain or suffering, which is in line with my spiritual beliefs. At one point, I went to a psychic medium who provided me with comfort and validation in my belief that Mahmoud and his brother were okay.

Admittedly, repeating these statements to myself didn't take away my pain altogether. I still wanted to share this incredible loss with my friends and family, so I wasn't carrying it alone. Unfortunately, very few people were able to meet my hope, so I tried counseling. Again, I was disappointed as I was generally met with the typical platitudes, 'I'm sorry for your loss' or painful stares. I needed acknowledgment that my heartache and horror were real. However, most people, including counselors, didn't know how to convey this. After his death, I also started to question whether I should continue in the counseling profession, particularly counseling other trauma survivors.

I remember asking myself, "Can I really do this? What else would you do if it wasn't holding others' pain?" I felt panicked and overwhelmed at the thought of leaving my profession because it was very much a part of my identity. In the end, what started to help me get through the horrific death of my friend was my group of Syrian friends or other "expats" who understood the terrible effects of war. I needed to be with others who understood what it felt like to lose a loved one in traumatic, sometimes unimaginable ways. I found great comfort in sharing my loss and learning how they were living with their own pain. Over time, their stories inspired me and gave me hope that I *could* and *should* continue to be a trauma counselor. I also came to realize this role would continue to heal my traumatic loss of Mahmoud. Personally and professionally, this is experienced as post-traumatic growth: growth experienced after your own difficult experience or witnessing the difficult experiences of others.

I still miss Mahmoud as much as I did when I learned he died. There continue to be certain images or thoughts about his death I don't allow myself to think about. I have learned to automatically replace those with the reminder he is not that person in pain or fear any longer. Even though several years have passed since Mahmoud was killed, when I cry, I don't judge myself for continuing to grieve him. There was a lot lost with the death of Mahmoud and his brother. To me, missing him is just a continued connection.

Anna's Story—The Day the Light Went Dim

In 2016, I tragically lost my mother to suicide after a long battle with mental health issues. Throughout my childhood, she had been in and out of inpatient hospitalizations, with ongoing struggles over the years. The difficulties she faced escalated when she experienced a house fire and separated from my stepfather within a short span of time. The combination of these stressors pushed her into a place of immense despair. Compounding the situation, I lived far away in a different state, and she lacked a strong local support network.

After several months of immense struggle, she had lost hope and was admitted to an inpatient hospital to treat her depression. While my mother had a few friends, she didn't have many family members she could rely on, so I took time off work and flew to her to step in to provide support when she was released. I accompanied her to intensive outpatient appointments, helped her around the house, and there were moments when it seemed like she had regained her sense of self. She was eating and talking more, and we were optimistic about her treatment. Shortly after her discharge, she went to a more intensive outpatient group. After her first day, she seemed like a ghost of herself. Unbeknownst to me, she had reached a point where she felt resigned and couldn't envision continuing her life any longer. I was devastated.

Initially, when confronted with sudden grief, it feels overwhelming, leaving you confused and helpless. It's as if a fog descends, erasing not only months but even years from memory. After taking a few days off work through bereavement leave, I realized I needed more time and sought assistance through the Family & Medical Leave Act (FMLA). Thankfully, my boss was understanding, granting me a month or so off work, during which I stayed in the vicinity of my mother's residence to sort out practical matters.

In the following years, I found myself aimlessly navigating through life, unsure of how to move forward. Initially, my focus was solely on managing daily essentials and making it work. I attempted to seek therapy, and while my therapist was compassionate, each session was permeated by my uncontrollable tears. I struggled to process my grief in a way that allowed closure. It never evolved into meaningful discussions but rather remained an open wound. Though my therapist understood the nature of grief, I felt disconnected, continuously losing sight of myself and unable to piece myself back together.

For a period of two to three years, I persisted with therapy until I stumbled upon a therapy group specifically tailored to sudden and traumatic loss. It was here that I felt a significant shift in my emotional state. While I had attended other support groups, sharing my story of loss often elicited gasps, as their experiences, while difficult, did not involve a sudden, traumatic event like mine. Consequently, I carried a sense of shame attached to my loss, hindering my ability to fully open up to those who couldn't comprehend the depth of my suffering. However, within this particular group, I found solace in discussing the intricate details of my experience with individuals who genuinely understood.

To this day, I am selective about whom I confide in regarding my loss. I find comfort in conversing with individuals who share a similar understanding. Within the therapy group I attended, several members had also lost someone to suicide, including those who had lost a parent in such a manner. This shared connection allowed for a deeper level of understanding and empathy. The most beneficial aspect was sharing my story and experiences with others who held a safe space for it. It wasn't solely the therapeutic techniques employed but the environment of support and understanding that truly aided in my healing process.

I believe these support groups offer tremendous value. They provide a space to process and alleviate the shame associated with our grief, allowing us to openly share our stories. Connecting with others who have undergone similar losses and maintaining contact with them has been invaluable.

There are moments when I find myself thinking, “Everything seems fine. I’m doing well.” However, grief has a way of resurfacing unexpectedly. It remains a constant presence in my life, never truly dissipating. Over time, I have learned to construct a life where grief doesn’t overpower everything and where it doesn’t entirely consume me.

As the years pass, the circle of grief gradually shrinks. Initially, it feels all-encompassing, overwhelming every aspect of existence. But as I began to engage in activities and experiences I once enjoyed, I noticed that my grief’s hold weakened. By actively pursuing a fulfilling life, the weight of grief lessens, and it feels like there is less sorrow.

Over time, I developed coping mechanisms and found ways to integrate grief into my life without allowing it to define me entirely. The loss became a part of my story, a chapter that shaped me, but it no longer dominated my thoughts and actions.

I haven’t really found that honoring anniversary dates was helpful for me. In the past, people would send me messages on the anniversary of her death, and I found it unsettling because I didn’t want that specific day to be associated with remembering her. In fact, I had to explicitly request that they refrain from texting me on that day because it isn’t something I really want to remember. Usually, I notice my mood change around the month of her birthday, and it always surprises me that I still have some trouble around that time.

The dynamic between my mother and me was incredibly complex. Although it may have seemed like we had a strong bond outwardly, the reality was far different. Our relationship was fraught with complications, and how others perceived it starkly contrasted with how I experienced it. This certainly impacted my grief process.

It's crucial to focus on getting through each day. Identify those individuals in your life who can serve as a reliable source of support, the ones you can confide in when you're feeling down and say, "I'm having a really tough day." Understand that some people might struggle with your emotions and find it uncomfortable, so finding those who can provide the understanding and empathy you need is essential. Recognize the importance of having someone who will remind you to take care of yourself, even during the darkest moments.

Fortunately, my husband was the person I could rely on the most during that period. For a year or two, I was unable to handle many responsibilities around the house, but he stepped in to ensure that I didn't have to face Everything alone. He made it a point to ensure I ate properly and cared for my basic needs.

Although he knew my mother, he wasn't hit with the loss as hard as I was, so it was difficult to connect with him about some of the hard stuff I was feeling and thinking. That's where the therapy group proved to be invaluable. It provided me with an outlet to share my thoughts and emotions with individuals who could truly empathize with my loss and ensure my well-being.

Jessica's Story—Walking Away

My fiancé and I were out to dinner with some of his family, discussing our wedding and having a cigar bar. We were going to have cigars and a whiskey pairing. I was trying to make it a big deal, and I didn't think I was, but I wanted it to be because, you know, it's my wedding day. My fiancé was just completely over it. He was completely over the conversation. He couldn't understand why we were talking about this. He thought guests should pick a cigar, grab whatever drink they wanted, and smoke it. I went on about how everything needed to look and be set up thematically. He thought I was being so extra. I never considered myself a bridezilla, but I was that one time. I was just so stuck on it.

On our drive home, my fiancé was super aggravated and annoyed with me that I couldn't let it go. He thought I was ruining the night. At first, I was silent in the car, and then I said something about it, and he pulled the car over on the side of the road. He had done this before. He got out of the car because he was just so mad at me. It was March, and our wedding was going to be in May. I thought to myself, "I'm not signing up for this. This is the third time he's done this to me where he has walked on the freeway away from me and just left me there, and I'm not going to do this."

I climbed over into the driver's seat. I didn't even look for him because he didn't come back the other times he did this. In the past, I would call him, find him, and beg for him to come back. But this time, I was just like, "I'm not. I won't. I'm done this time. I'm done. He's got to make this right." The car was parked on the side of the road, just 5 minutes from my home. That's the thing. We weren't even that far away from the house. Like, just get to the house, you know? And yell at me there about cigars and whiskey.

I went home, went to bed, and I woke up the next morning at around 5:00 a.m., and he wasn't in bed. I went downstairs, and he wasn't there. I started calling his cell phone. Then I went out to the car to see if he'd taken it. But it was there, and so was his phone. So then I Google, "What do you do when you don't know where someone is?" He didn't have an Apple Watch or anything else I could use to locate him, so I started calling hospitals, and then I started Googling police stations, and I just sat there. Then, at 6:00 or 7:00 in the morning, I get a call from his dad. He said, "Were you out with Jason last night?" And I said, "Yeah." Then he asked, "Were you in Bend?" I told him that it was on our way home. And then he just said, "Jason is dead." I said, "What?" And he said again, "Jason is dead." That's when the shrieking started, and I just started sobbing. His dad said, "I'm sorry." It didn't feel like he meant that he felt sorry for the loss of Jason but that he was sorry that he had to call and tell me like this.

I called my mother because we were supposed to have my first dress alteration that day, and no one answered at my parent's house. I started panicking and called my brother. He was driving, and I told him what happened, and I don't know how he didn't get in an accident. He just started screaming. Then I called one of my best friends, who was my maid of honor, and she came over. My parents called me next and also came over.

I remember the first person who came to the door was a chaplain from the police station. It was some old white lady who just really believed in God, and the last thing I needed was anyone telling me that there was a God at that moment. She wanted to sit down and talk to me, and all I could think was, "Why are you here? Of all the people I need in my life, it is not some random person."

The coroner was the one who called Jason's dad. I called the coroner, telling him that I was Jason's fiancé. The coroner said they couldn't identify him besides having his wallet and driver's license and asked if Jason had any identifiable marks on his body, tattoos, or anything like that. I said, "No, Jason didn't have tattoos. But he had kidney surgery when he was a kid. So he has a pretty long kidney scar on his left side." The coroner asked, "Anything else?" I was confused. The scar was pretty big. It was like 12 inches long. Wouldn't that be enough to identify him? Then I said, "He had a nipple ring on his right nipple years ago and it got ripped out, so that nipple looks different." And the coroner said, "Okay, yes, this is him."

I found out later from his brother, and I guess people say things like this because they're idiots and don't know what they're saying, but that week, he came over and said, "You know, they had to, like, pick up Jason's shoes because the bus hit him so hard that his shoes fell off and the bus just dragged his body." I realized that's why the coroner didn't see the scar on his left side because he had been dragged by the bus so hard that he didn't know what he looked like. I asked the coroner for his fingerprints and found a shop on Etsy that could make a necklace with an impression of his fingerprints. I remember holding that necklace so that it didn't seem as weird that he wasn't there. So that everywhere I could always just be touching and rubbing it, and it would be him.

My family came, my friends came. Everyone just started showing up. Every day, someone new showed up from my life to console me, and I just started sobbing like I just found out all over again. I had so many phone calls I don't remember from whom. I remember the day it got real because there were always people in the house. I sat in the corner of the couch in the living room in the same clothes. My mother would beg me to let her wash my sweatshirt and leggings because that's all I'd wear.

The house got really quiet, and my kid brother kept going in and out of the house to take a call. One of the reporters had put in the papers that I was responsible for the accident and that I was the "woman he was with." That's how I was referred to. I found out later that my brother was taking calls from the detective because he was trying to protect me.

I remember his parents coming over the first time, sitting on the couch, and hugging me. Then they started asking for passwords to his bank accounts and financial things, and it made me so mad I stood up, walked away, and went upstairs. I literally don't even know why we were talking about it. His family wrote his obituary and forgot to include me. I know we were all struggling, but I was eight weeks away from being the person who would have had full responsibility for managing everything.

Jason died in March, and it was probably May when I first reached out to find help. I contacted a couple of therapy groups and was told it was too early. I thought to myself, "What is too early? I don't know what to do with myself!" It had been two months of me sitting on the couch in the same clothes. Not moving, barely sleeping. My best friend had been here for three weeks. I don't remember being able to do anything or feel anything. People gave me all the books. I was reading books. "It's Okay That You're Not Okay" by Megan Devine was the only one that seemed decent. It felt similar because of the loss.

What was most helpful for me was the trauma therapy group I participated in and listening to stories from other group members. It helped me remember some of those moments in the beginning because they remembered, and I don't know how they remembered. I remember listening to another woman's story and sharing about getting the phone call about the person she lost and the earth-shattering screams she experienced. I started hyperventilating and had to walk out to get fresh air.

I had the most amazing boss in the world. Being in HR (human resources), you know all the rules. I knew I was eligible for leave under FMLA (Family and Medical Leave Act), but it was a small company, so we didn't have many extra benefits besides a guarantee of employment. But there wasn't a question; I wasn't coming into work, but I wasn't getting docked pay either. I wasn't on FMLA. I wasn't taking vacation time. I was just getting paid.

My boss slowly reintroduced me back to work, starting with a project I helped her with. I worked with the most amazing people. I had been with that company for 13 years, so everyone knew me. Everyone knew everything about me. The CEO and many supervisors and managers had shown up to the memorial. On my first day back at work, I remember thinking, "I don't want to walk in because people are going to look at me." So when I got to the parking lot the first day, I remember crying. One of my teammates, a dear friend, worked it out so I would have someone to go with me whenever I needed to walk to or from my car. Whenever I needed to use the restroom, somebody would accompany me so that nobody would talk to me.

I remember my mother begging me to eat. I ate cheese toast. A piece of toast with a piece of cheese on it. Not even a grilled cheese sandwich. Cheese toast was the best I could do. And I still couldn't lose weight. My body said, "Nope, we're gonna hold on to everything," because I was completely shut down.

I went to the doctor for sleep medications, trying "Calm" and trying to figure out what to do to fall asleep. I got anxiety medication. It was the first time in my life that I ever felt the need for that. The doctor didn't want to prescribe me Xanax, and instead, he prescribed Propranolol because it's softer and doesn't have the rebound effect. It was like having the feather in Dumbo's hat. Like having it was enough. I would experience episodes where my heart would be so tight I couldn't breathe. Most of the time, I figured out that it would go away if somebody just started talking about anything else. But it was learning to ride the waves. I didn't know how to do that back then.

One of my friends got me a weighted blanket, and it might have helped me get some sleep because I was just a zombie of a human. I don't really recall anything. I had to go back to live at my house, and it was difficult to stay there alone, so some of my girlfriends would come and stay with me for a couple of nights. They'd leave their families and go and stay with me. My boss was based in another state, and she would stay with me instead of staying in a hotel when she would come up for work. Every part of that house was Jason. I had owned it before him, but it was our house. There was just stuff everywhere. Jason was a collector of everything. Everything was in multiples, so there was just so much stuff to clean up.

So, I had to be okay with anxiety medication. I had to be okay with some sleep aids because I wasn't really sleeping. I have no idea what I did. I was just like a blob, and then, at some point, I said I needed help, and there were no resources. There was nobody to talk to. I think it was in June that I found a grief therapist who ended up being near the home that Jason and I had shared, and I remember trying to navigate that. When the therapist called me, I told her I needed help and just started crying. She was completely booked but was able to get me an appointment within a couple of weeks.

I wore my engagement ring a lot back then. I would hear people say, "You're just so strong." I don't know what that means. I don't know what the other option is. I don't remember what I did in those first two months, but I knew I couldn't keep being that version of myself.

I just felt like I needed a handbook. I needed somebody to tell me what to do, and everybody just told me, "Time." And I'm like, "Thanks. What do you want me to do with that?" People would ask, "What are you supposed to do?" and I didn't know what I was supposed to do. They would ask, "How can I help?" and I would say, "I literally have no idea. I don't know." They would ask, "What do you want?" and I would say, "I don't know." Someone asked me, "Do you want to go get your hair done?" I said, "I don't care what I look like. Does anybody care what I look like? Nobody cares. The person that cared what I look like isn't here anymore." Nothing mattered.

The relationship with his family never got any better. My mother recently admitted to me that she had seen Jason's parents. Our families grew up a mile apart. So they would see my mother and ask for things, and she told them not to stop by and not to contact me if all they wanted were things. They would only contact our family when they wanted something. Once in a while, I see his mom's car, and I have a moment of panic. Sometimes, I thought I should stop by his parent's house to give them something I thought they should have, but I couldn't open that door. I can't open that wound because it doesn't feel like it's going to be healthy. It just feels like a wound.

I've always had a hard time with the day and the date. The accident happened on a Friday night. The day will come, and not that I would forget, but I wouldn't understand the emotions that are brewing. The brain fog would come on heavy that week. If I didn't write it down, don't even pretend to ask me if I did it because I won't know. I will forget when I spoke to people. That's been consistent for the last five years. Brain fog the week coming up to it and the week after. I've told my boss that having a "To-Do List" is the only thing I'm capable of doing during that time. I can't figure my way out of it. On the Friday Jason died, we went early to have a drink before dinner because it was sunny, and a sunny March day where we live is not very common. And now, every Friday right around that date is always sunny. It's been sunny every year since. It blows my mind.

I had been avoiding the area where we lived on the date itself. I've been flying out of state to my brother's house. I did it last year. This year, my boyfriend said he asked if we could stay here. He said we didn't have to do anything but asked if we could try. So I agreed, and I told him I'd like to go to Jason's grave, and I wanted him to bring his dog since I don't have mine anymore. I was already on edge, not realizing I was on edge, and I was busy at work that day. The graveyard was closing at 5:00 p.m., and I called my boyfriend on my way to pick him up. There was traffic, and I was crying and carrying on, thinking I wouldn't make it in time. He said he would take care of getting flowers and told me just to come and pick him up, and we would go.

The cemetery is located on the top of a hill, and on a pretty day, you can see mountains and the water, which were Jason's things, which is why I put them there. I keep a scrub brush, water bottle, and towel in my car, so the first thing I did was clean his headstone. Why did no one tell me I needed an upright headstone, not a flat one? It's a disaster. I have to clean it all the time. It always has grass trimmings on it. So I'm sitting down on my knees, scrubbing and cleaning it, and my boyfriend and his dog are sitting quietly behind me, and I'm talking to Jason. Then, all of a sudden, this cathartic, overwhelming, deep cry that I didn't know I still had in me just came out. I was sobbing. Sobbing. It had been five years. Then I introduced him to my boyfriend and his dog while my boyfriend held my hand.

One day, I was talking about Jason more than usual, and my boyfriend asked me why because he wanted to make sure I was doing okay. It's weird because, in these spaces and these relationships, we're not talking about an ex. We're talking about someone who died. And they're not perfect, and we know they weren't perfect, but they gain a level of perfection in death because they are put on a pedestal, and we get to forget about all the stupid things they did, and we get to talk about them. And I believe the only way you can find that next person is if they're okay with hearing it and never throwing it in your face. Maybe it's not the most comfortable thing for them, but it wasn't the most comfortable thing for us to deal with either. So when I talked about Jason, it didn't feel weird, and I don't think it felt weird for my boyfriend. He was just curious as to why I was telling all these stories, and I don't know why other than I was in a good spot and felt like talking about him.

Sometimes, something will fall down in the house, and I'll say, "Hi, Jason. I see you." I was the only one in the trauma therapy group who believed in that. Everyone else was skeptical. What's the harm in letting yourself believe that? That somebody's going to call you stupid? Somebody's going to give you advice on 18 different things, and you're going to ignore them on that too. But for me, there's nothing that doesn't feel good about it. A woman in my group had lost her sister, and she started saying "Hi" to her sister every time something fell down in her house. She said it felt so good to acknowledge her that way, and I assured her it was okay.

About four months after Jason passed, I went to a medium. I didn't give them any information about us. Because of what was happening in the news, my friends got online and deleted the wedding registries and anything else that connected our names to protect me from being identified. So I was sitting there with the medium, and everything she said was basic, but anything felt good in those moments. But then she said, "He keeps saying something, and it's odd, and I don't know what to do with it. But he just keeps repeating it, so I have to tell you," and then she said, "He's saying something about socks." I love goofy socks. So I have socks everywhere. I have my hiking and sports socks, and there's no space for more socks. I have an entire cabinet full of socks. Jason had to buy me another drawer. I had so many socks. So, I knew that was him.

Later on, I went to a psychic. Religious people will say, “Everyone has their day.” The psychic told me the opposite and said it wasn’t his day. He wasn’t supposed to leave. He’s stuck. He still loves you. That was the stuck piece. I was feeling him so much, and with me where I was in my grief at the time, my mother kept telling me to tell him, “It’s okay to go to the light. It’s okay.” Because it felt like he was stuck in-between. I would think that for as much crap as Jason did, he’s still going to heaven because he’s entertaining, and he’ll be the nature guide for everyone else when he gets up there. When our dog would be “running” in his sleep, I knew he was up there running with Daddy. When things like that happened, I embraced it.

Somehow, I found The Dinner Party, a virtual meeting space for people who are grieving a loss. I wanted to join because I felt like that type of connection was a piece I was missing. But I had zero interest in a relationship at that time. The group had some fiancés and widows. Most people in the group had lost someone to an illness. Everyone except one girl in the group said that the remedy for your grief is to “get under someone.” Just have sex again. I was so confused. I thought, “Did you guys even like your person?” The last thing I wanted to do was be touched by somebody. I couldn’t understand. Why would I? Why would I want that? Why would I want to kiss someone? But men do it all the time. When men lose somebody, they immediately get into a relationship again. I get that. I hear you. And yes, I'm judging you, but it's just not for me. It's just not my way.

About 2½ years ago, I realized I was ready to date again. So I started getting on some apps and trying online dating, just talking to people. I clarified my intentions and boundaries when I told my family about it. I told them I was going to do this, but I'm a grown woman, and I wasn't going to come home to tell them how it was. I'm not going to tell them where I went. Someone will know where I am because I've always been that way, but it will not be anyone in the family. And when I come home at night, it doesn't matter the hour because I am 40 plus years old.

When I knew I was ready to meet someone else, I felt like my dog (keep in mind this was Jason's dog that became our dog) knew I needed to close a chapter. After a lengthy battle with cancer, my dog passed away. It was like he closed one chapter so I could open another one clean. I had just met my boyfriend then, so how it happened was very ceremonious. I guess it was where we were supposed to be. When he and I first started dating, he told me he had been going to therapy and said I was "So clean." He complimented me on how much work I had done to navigate my grief and gave me the space to know when those moments were. But I still have those anxiety pills, and I take them now. They probably would have been helpful in life before what happened. You know, like before a presentation at work. If I take one, I'm so much better and feel better about presenting.

Unfortunately, as soon as you become part of the "group" (someone who has lost someone traumatically), you find more people who are part of the group. Somebody has asked me for resources at least once a year in the last five years because something traumatic just happened to them. You can't hand them a therapist right at that moment but have this resource, and in a couple of months, you can remind them it's there. Some friends set up a meal schedule for me that ran for two weeks after Jason passed away. My best girlfriends moved in with me. I had friends who would visit me every day. My table was always full. There were just people here. My mother is skittish around animals, and my dog always scared her, but she came around anyway and would protect and love him.

My parents commented that the friends I had around me were impressive because everyone just showed up. I didn't have to make as many decisions or look for as many resources because there were humans there that would say, "Are you okay?" My paychecks didn't stop. I didn't have to worry about paying a mortgage on a house I wasn't living in. I didn't have car payments. I didn't have medical expenses. I had people to protect me when Jason's family would stop by and ask stupid things or make stupid requests. I'm thankful for that because, in my state of mind, I would have given my Social Security Number and date of birth to anyone who asked for it. I would have done anything, but people always watched out for me. There is a piece of this that feels very selfish. I didn't realize how much I had that surrounded me. That's the hard part, especially for those who don't have that level of support around them.

The reality is no matter what anyone thinks, we all need therapy. Small groups like the trauma therapy group that I was in are important. It's important to go through. The only thing that would make it better is if the group could offer resources afterward to keep group members connected with therapists monthly, with therapists who can offer sliding scales and things like that for people who don't have insurance. Other things would come up after I stopped meeting with the group, and it would have been beneficial to talk to the therapist from my group about it. I would want to talk to Jason about things like having work issues or getting in a fight with my family and my dad sticking up for my mom and not having anyone to stick up for me, or having a dog to have the warmth in bed because it's like having someone there.

Knowing it's okay to yell at somebody when they say you're strong and not biting your tongue every single time. Okay, somebody gets a paper cut because your tongue was too sharp. You're not a bad person. People don't know what to say, but sometimes you don't have to listen to or acknowledge every stupid thing that people do say. I have the most kindhearted lovely friends in the world and one that is very, very Christian, and I have told them, "It was *not* his day. I need you to stop saying that." If everyone were born with a day, I'd like to speak with the person up there with the calendar! That comment made me feel lost in my faith. I didn't want to go to church.

One of the books I read was “Option B” by Sheryl Sandberg. She shares some good points, but I was a little on the fence about it only because she got into a relationship faster than I would, and when I was reading it, I thought, “What am I missing?” I might just be being judgemental. But it’s important to remember that no one is going to have your experience. Everyone has their season. You have to be able to take what resonates with you from that piece and then burn the rest.

Nature is 100% a thing. Get outside, sit outside, and go for a walk. It doesn’t require money or having a big backyard. Get some fresh air. No one is going to have the solution for you, and you don’t have to be strong. You can melt into the ground some days, but it’s what picks you back up that’s important. What navigates that wave? I can see it in my head when I’m in it. I’m holding my breath with the surfboard, going underneath the wave, and asking myself, “How am I getting back up?” This one’s deep. It’s the rocking chair. Some days, you don’t know what day it is. I don’t remember an entire year. And life keeps going on.

I don’t know how you make this better. There just aren’t a lot of resources. You have to be willing to dig and have the space and opportunity to do it. As I recall, a friend of my brother, a therapist, gave me the resources to start making the calls I did. I didn’t even know where to look. That’s what the chaplain and coroner should be doing, providing resources that can be tucked away and used later. It’s nothing you’ll pay attention to now, but you may need those resources 60 days, 90 days, or six months later. I don't know how the people who don't have people to support them do it. Some relationships and family relationships are more strained, and maybe that's why it takes longer to get to therapy. They don't realize they need it. There's still anger. My family still has a lot of anger for what Jason did. I don't know what life is supposed to teach us, but this is a lesson I didn't want to learn.

I found this organization where you can donate hiking and camping clothes for underprivileged youth, and it was perfect because most of his clothes were like athletic wear. We had just gone to REI (Recreational Equipment, Inc.) before Jason passed away, so I had all these clothes. It was an excellent opportunity to give his clothes away that way instead of donating them to a generic donation center. It was cathartic. I remember pulling dirty laundry out of the basket with his sweat and cologne, putting it in a zip-lock bag, opening it up occasionally, and smelling it. I would put on some of his cologne and smell it. Sometimes, I'd wear his cologne, and my dog would lick the spot where his cologne was because it smelled like Daddy. That kind of stuff you do when you're ready, and no one knows but you when the time is right.

Daniel's Story—No Accident

It seems like yesterday that I could hear her laugh, the one from the depth of her gut that would just command the room. But, in 2015, I lost my sister, who her boyfriend killed in a car crash. And I don't say car accident on purpose. That's intentional because it wasn't an accident. The crash happened right next to her apartment building, and her boyfriend was drunk and high on drugs, driving between 70 and 80 miles an hour down a neighborhood street with a speed limit of 25 miles per hour. The car spun out of control and crashed into a large green electrical box and my sister was thrown from the car, and the car landed on top of her.

She took her last breath at that moment, and I am here to make sure her story doesn't go untold.

I got a phone call from my mom at 5:00 in the morning, and I didn't answer it because I was asleep. She left a voicemail that said, "Hey, it's your mom. Could you please call me back?" She was talking in one of those low-tone, quiet voices that made me think this was not a good phone call. I called her back about ten times, and she didn't answer, so I called my dad. He answered and said, "Your sister has been in a really bad car accident, Daniel, and she died." My sister was a single mom with two kids, who were seven and thirteen at the time and were sitting there with my dad. It was at that moment I realized the unconditional love and support those boys would need from then on.

After I heard the news, I was so shocked and torn up that I went and woke up my partner at the time now husband, and told him what happened, got in the car, and raced down to the scene. Everything was still going on. The car was still there, and it seemed like the world was moving in slow motion with all the silence, disbelief, wonder, and tears. The scene of the crash was under investigation, with evidence being marked and police conversing about their report. My sister's body was already gone. And then, we had to deal with the aftermath while trying to grieve and care for two boys who lost their mom.

My sister's boyfriend was an egregious criminal with a long record, and the crash was his third strike, and he got life in prison—a trial that took several years, but when I walked out of the courtroom on the sentencing day, I was so relieved—that was it, we were done … or so I thought. Unfortunately, after almost eight years since the crash, we had to go back to court a couple of months ago because recent changes to state laws have reduced sentences for criminals for certain crimes, and his sentence was reduced. I stood up in court and read a statement, and the first thing I said was, "I would rather be anywhere else in the world than standing here in this courtroom, looking at the man who killed my sister."

When the crash happened, it was highly publicized because the Department of Corrections had made a mistake, and my sister's boyfriend was released early for another crime he had committed, and he should not have been out of jail when my sister was killed. That's another element that became part of the criminal and civil proceedings.

Then, there was finding a place for my sister's kids to live. All of a sudden, they had to move in with their grandparents and start therapy, and getting all of that situated was a whole other journey in and of itself. I feel like within this whole story, there are all these micro-stories and so many things we had to do, which is probably not unlike other people's experiences in these situations, and we tried to navigate it all the best we could, and it wasn't easy.

I remember a lot of sitting and crying by myself. I would cry a lot when I was driving alone. For some reason, I wouldn't allow myself to cry in front of other people. I have two blood-related siblings—my sister who died and another sister with whom I don't really have a relationship. And my parents got divorced a long, long time ago. So, the only other person who really understood was my mom, who I felt could go through the grief journey with me.

There were little things that helped me, like when my stepdad and I went and cleaned out my sister's apartment, which I really didn't want to do, but it ended up being really therapeutic because I felt like I got to help do something for her and honor her life by helping to close a chapter. But a lot of times, I would call my mom, and we would just cry together. We would ask each other, "Why did this happen?" Sometimes, we would just be silent, which was OK because of our connection with my sister. But it was still such a weird feeling. Sometimes, I would call my sister's phone just in case this was a dream, hoping she would answer.

Honestly, I didn't really know what to do until I heard about a grief therapy group from the victim's advocate through the prosecutor's office, and I decided that's what I would do. I firmly believe there was no better choice I could have made in my entire life. Part of my story is that my sister got wrapped up with some bad people and went down this path of living a life where she made some poor choices due to her own feelings of insecurity and self-doubt, but it's not at all how I feel like we were raised. She and I were very different in terms of our paths in life, which made me nervous because I thought the members of the group might judge me, but there was no judgment amongst these angels on Earth, which I will share more about in a bit.

So, I was a little scared to go to the grief group because I thought I would receive a lot of judgment. I did what the attorneys told me not to do, and I read the comments to the newspaper articles about my sister's crash, and my, oh my, are people quick to judge. There were comments like, "She deserved to die." or, "I think she should have died." All written by these trolls who didn't know anything. I don't know why I read them because it was so depressing. It compounded this feeling of judgment that I thought I would feel walking into the grief therapy group where I would say something like, "My sister was on the news because she was dating this guy that was in jail, and this happened." I worried I would be judged because of my sister's situation and how she died, and I am so grateful that was not the case.

Much to my relief, my experience with the grief therapy group was totally the opposite of what I thought it would be. I walked into that room on the first day and knew I was in the right spot. I sat down and just started crying, looking at all these people who were complete strangers because it was a tangible feeling in that small room in that circle we were sitting in that these people were going to get it. These people are going to be supportive, and these people are going to share their story that's going to be like my story and validate it, and I'm going to learn from them, and they're going to learn from me, and we're going to get through it together.

That was the beginning of navigating my grief, but grief is never-ending and unexpectedly percolates back up to the top. In my case, we are not only dealing with a criminal trial but also a civil trial. So the victim's advocate would call me and tell me there's a court date being set, and then the court date changes, or it's canceled, then it's next month. In my mind, this is never-ending. There will probably be another court date surrounding my sister's death. But I am hoping the most recent one was the last.

I hold a lot of the heaviness in my heart about my sister's boys. They have different dads who are not in the picture, so neither of my nephews had parents for some time. The younger one now lives with his dad and stepmom, but the older one hasn't had any parents since he was 13, so I experience wafts of guilt in terms of the "what-ifs" and "should haves" that I feel never really help anyone's psyche. I would ask myself, "Should I have moved them into my house?" "Should I have done something I wasn't doing because these poor kids lost their mom?" "Should I have done … more."

My older nephew heard the crash because it was so close to home, and he ran down and saw his mom dead underneath the car and touched her. I still think about the trauma that came from that for my nephew. It throws your brain for a loop when you're that age and lose your mom. So I'm just trying to be there for them. They're fifteen and twenty-one now, and I have the younger one over for a weekend every month, so that's nice. He texts me every weekend to ask me what I'm doing, and I am so grateful I get to be a part of his adolescent life.

One really neat thing that happened when my sister died was that all of a sudden, all of these random people were reaching out to us, and we didn't know who they were, but they just wanted to help, and they were being so nice. Well, lo and behold, we discovered they were part of my sister's neighborhood Buy Nothing group, which is a group where you can give or receive items from your neighbors that are no longer wanted or needed for free. So all of these lovely people came together and just wanted to help our family in any way. They wanted to help clean up my sister's apartment and help give stuff away and things like that, and they were just the nicest people. I had never heard of Buy Nothing before, but I got to know them, and they came over to my parent's house and would check in with us a lot. They would ask us about the court dates and wanted to be there for support. So, my sister had this little community within her neighborhood.

One thing I decided to do was to learn more about Buy Nothing. So, I joined the group in my neighborhood and eventually became an administrator because I thought that was a neat little way for me to continue to feel connected to my sister. She was a huge part of her Buy Nothing group, and it was one small way for me to feel like she and I were doing something together to carry on her spirit.

I was the last person in my family to see my sister alive on the day of the crash, which I am eternally grateful for because life is short, sacred, and precious. My last memory of my sister is embedded in my heart and soul, and I am so grateful. We all know this and say this all the time, but I think the trajectory of my healing and dealing with this sudden traumatic loss in my life and my family's life would have been very different if my relationship with my sister had not been good at the end of her life. So I felt really good about the fact on her last day on Earth, the last thing I did was hug her and tell her I loved her. We laughed and embraced, which really does carry me through because that's my last lasting memory of her. She had a big smile on her face, and we took a picture together, which was nice. We casually say it all the time, but I really believe you should never go to bed in a fight and always tell your friends and family how much you love them.

Sometimes, things will happen that are little nuggets of knowing that I still have a connection with my sister. Recently, I took my nephew to an event, and on the way back, we were about to pass the exit to where my sister's apartment was, and my nephew asked, "Hey, Uncle, do you mind if we go drive by my old house?" And I said, "Yeah, totally. We can totally drive by there, and I'm so happy to drive by there, but you'll see your old house, and you'll see the scene of the accident," to which he replied, "I really want to go." So we drove by there. We've also visited her where she's buried, where her ashes are.

My sister really liked going to The Cheesecake Factory, and she would take her kids there a lot and meet up with us there. So on her birthday most years, we go to The Cheesecake Factory together. I have a tattoo in remembrance of her with birds on a wire that represents our family, with one of the birds flying away that represents my sister, and above and below the wire, it says, "Sister, you are free" in Morse code. I think my sister was a little bit trapped in her own mind when she was on Earth, and I do feel like she's free now and happier in some senses.

The biggest takeaway still for me that I'm working through to this day is, "What will be will be." There's no prescription to get grief right for yourself or for taking care of other people, either. If you do the best you can with the information you have, in the best way you know how to take care of yourself and love other people who miss the person who was lost in your life, that is good enough. That is exactly what you should be doing.

I don't think it's possible to move forward if you're constantly second-guessing yourself like, "Oh, I should have done that" or "Oh, I should have done this." I had a really good last interaction with my sister, which has significantly helped my healing journey. But even for folks that that wasn't the case, I don't think our loved ones who we lost would want us to beat ourselves up about anything. I think my sister is whispering in my ear, "Thank you for loving my kids. Thank you for being there for my kids. Thank you for being an awesome brother. I have Nothing but love for you, and you've done it perfectly." I think she would tell me, "You're doing everything perfectly." Even when there are times when I'm like, "Oh, should I do that? Or should I send them to this school? Or should we hire this tutor?" Or like throwing money at the problem or buying a better present. Little things go through my head, like, "Oh, they lost their mom. I should take them to the fancier restaurant." But what we do is enough. All her kids want is love and care and to feel normalcy and stability. And that's good enough.

DISCLAIMER

The author of this book is not a doctor, lawyer, or financial advisor, or other qualified professional. The content is for informational purposes only and should not replace legal, medical, financial, or other professional advice. You should seek the assistance of a professional before making any significant decisions or taking any actions based on what you read in this book.

The resources referenced in this book, including but not limited to all websites, products, and services, are for informational purposes only. Any decision to purchase or utilize them will be at the reader's discretion and risk. The author does not endorse nor have they been compensated for endorsing any of the resources mentioned in this book. It is important to conduct research before deciding to utilize or purchase them. In addition, the resources listed in this book may have changed or no longer be valid or exist between when it was written and when it was read.

The names of individuals mentioned in this book have been changed to protect their identities and maintain their anonymity. This decision was made so that their personal experiences, stories, contributions, privacy, and confidentiality were respected.

This book is intended to be informative, thought-provoking, and inspiring but is not a substitute for professional help. Everyone's situation is unique, and the information in this book may not apply to your specific situation or circumstances. The author, editor, and publisher are not liable for damages due to decisions made based on the content of this book.

ACKNOWLEDGMENTS

I want to extend my heartfelt gratitude and appreciation to each incredible individual who has contributed to this book, both directly and indirectly. Your unwavering support and encouragement have been instrumental in making it a reality. Your belief in me has sustained me and guided me throughout this transformative journey, and you have been a constant source of inspiration. Your enthusiasm motivated me to push forward, even when it got challenging and I debated giving up. It helped remind me of why I started writing this in the first place: to help people.

Sadly, this book would not exist had it not been for a tragedy. A tragedy that affected so many of you who have been on this journey with me since day one. You were alongside me through those horrific first few hours, numbing first days, sleepless weeks, and agonizing months. To those who made sure I slept, ate, helped me pack and move, drove me to appointments, were patient with me when I wasn't present, included me, took care of me, lent a listening ear, a shoulder to cry on, and allowed me to grieve without judgment, I thank you from the bottom of my heart.

Thank you to the many professionals, colleagues, and friends who, because of your expertise, I managed many administrative processes far better than I could have on my own. Your patience and understanding when I had so many questions was so appreciated. Because of you, I can share tips and suggestions that will be helpful for others struggling with similar situations, and that is invaluable.

To the anonymous contributors who have significantly influenced this work, I am forever grateful for your bravery in opening up and sharing your stories with the world. I empathize with what it takes to reopen wounds, and I do not doubt that your words will speak to so many who need to hear them. You have enriched this book in unimaginable ways, and I am honored to have you as a part of this journey. I am confident that you will be helpful to so many who will empathize with and relate to your honest, raw, and candid contributions.

I want to thank the team and fellow authors at Global Book Publishing, whose guidance and mentorship have been indispensable. Your insights and expertise helped me create something beyond what I could have imagined.

Lastly, I would like to express my gratitude to my readers. Your engagement and interest make all the hours, days, and years I've put into this worthwhile. I hope this book proves to be a valuable and comforting resource for you, and I am honored to have you join me on this journey.

ABOUT THE AUTHOR

Jennifer Nilsen is a widow, marketing professional, grief and loss discussion advocate, and author of "*An Unwanted Journey: Embracing Life After Loss*," which she wrote after the untimely and unexpected loss of her husband. Due to his passing, she was suddenly thrown into managing many complex and challenging transactions and processes while trying to navigate her grief. She felt compelled to share her story with the hope that it would be helpful to others.

Get in touch with author at:

- @jennifernilsenauthor
- @jennifernilsenauthor
- www.linkedin.com/company/jennifer-nilsen-author
- contact@jennifernilsenauthor.com

Made in the USA
Monee, IL
16 February 2024

bf03982b-84b2-4db1-ad63-0f605805e935R01